MY MOTHER SAID I NEVER SHOULD

Charlotte Keatley

Published by Methuen Drama
in association with Oxford Stage Company

Methuen Drama Modern Plays

10 9 8 7

First published in Great Britain in 1988
by Methuen London Ltd
Reprinted with revisions 1989, 1990
This revised edition published 1997 by
Methuen Publishing Limited
Reprinted in 2006 by Methuen Drama
A & C Black Publishers Limited
38 Soho Square
London W1D 3HB

Copyright © 1988, 1989, 1990, 1997 by Charlotte Keatley

Introduction © 1997 by Charlotte Keatley

A CIP catalogue record for this book is available from the
British Library

ISBN 978-0-413-71610-1

Typeset by Wilmaset Ltd, Birkenhead, Wirral
Printed and bound in Great Britain by
Cox & Wyman Ltd, Reading, Berkshire

OXFORD STAGE COMPANY

My Mother Said I Never Should
by Charlotte Keatley

Directed by Dominic Cooke

Designed by Robert Innes Hopkins

Lighting Designed by Paul Russell

Music composed by Gary Yershon

Movement direction by Liz Ranken

My Mother Said I Never Should was premiered at the
Contact Theatre, Manchester on 25 February 1987.
A revised version had its premiere at the
Royal Court Theatre, London on 23 February 1989.

31 Jan-8 Feb HUDDERSFIELD Lawrence Batley Theatre

11-15 Feb OXFORD Playhouse

18-22 Feb BUXTON Opera House

22 Feb-1 Mar BURY ST EDMUNDS Theatre Royal

4-8 Mar COVENTRY Warwick Arts Centre

12-15 Mar BRIGHTON Gardner Arts Centre

19-22 Mar TAUNTON Brewhouse Theatre & Arts Centre

25-29 Mar DARLINGTON Civic Theatre

1-5 Apr STIRLING MacRobert Arts Centre

8-12 Apr MANCHESTER Library Theatre

15-19 Apr CHELTENHAM Everyman Theatre

22-26 Apr LIVERPOOL Everyman Theatre

7-31 May LONDON Young Vic

 THE ARTS COUNCIL OF ENGLAND

 FINANCIALLY SUPPORTED BY OXFORDSHIRE COUNTY COUNCIL

 OXFORD CITY COUNCIL LEISURE SERVICES

Before rehearsals began, playwright Charlotte Keatley and director Dominic Cooke discussed their thinking behind the current production of My Mother Said I Never Should.

CK: Why do you want to direct this play?

DC: I've wanted to direct the play since I first read it eight years ago. It was an immediate gut response to the central theme of the play: the theme of emotional inheritance. I was very moved by it. The great strength of the play is that it deals in archetypes, which we can all recognise. Especially in the child scenes.

CK: How will you approach these scenes?

DC: To me the children are the centre of the play. The adults in the play wear masks, but when we see the children we see those people as they really are: saying what they mean and genuinely exploring the world. So it's not about putting on a childish voice and looking cute, but about finding the person that the adult has locked away. To do that we will draw on the actors' own experience of how it felt to look at the world as a five or an eight year old.

CK: Do you see it as a political play?

DC: Absolutely. We see how intensely four people react to all the changes and values of this century and the ideals of their generation. We examine the political through the personal choices that people make, how people live, not theories or abstract ideas.

CK: How do you feel as a man directing this play?

DC: To me, theatre's about imagination and neither gender has a monopoly on that. Would we say that a woman can never direct a Shakespeare play? Turning the tables, how do you feel having the play directed by a man?

CK: I wouldn't want to write a play that could only be directed by a woman, that would be like writing a play that only a woman could understand. In this play what the women are dreaming and hoping about is essential and universal. Am I going to get married or not? Have a child or not? Have a job or not? Concerns that are common to many of us. Women can sometimes hold back their own art unintentionally, by seeing it as belonging to women, instead of projecting it out as mainstream art for all of us, in which the women are the story tellers.

DC: And there are male characters in the play. We may not see them, but their presence is strongly felt.

CK: Yes - I wanted to examine the way women react to the men they have attatchments to: the husbands, fathers and boyfriends. This way, we learn about the expectations of the male society around them, the pressure to be "good women of their time".

DC: And the men are only trying to fulfil the expectation of a "good man" at that moment. Jack, Doris' husband, is being a good husband and father of the time. Working very hard, covering up his vulnerability. He's not intentionally cruel. But why was it so important to keep the men off stage?

CK: Because on stage, we see how women often have higher expectations of themselves than men. I wanted to focus on our responsibility, as women, to let go of certain expectations. I think society is still balanced towards men in employment, education, politics, industry, media... I wanted to get the women on stage and look at how we're handling that imbalance. And I wanted to put on stage the key occupation of women, which is still completely undervalued in our society, being a mother.

DC: How has it been to see so many different productions around the world?

CK: I have no favourite production. People often think that I have a perfect version in my head and go around measuring their production against it. I could see the same production on two different nights, and on one might think "we got that bit right tonight" and the next night, it won't get to me.

DC: How does it feel to come back to the play ten years after it was first performed?

CK: It's a really good moment to come back to it. My life is passing along some of the experiences of the play: I'm now married and I've got a child. In a strange way, I'm better equipped to look at my own play. Also, I feel we're finding a deeper meaning of the play now, as opposed to what it meant in Germany three years ago, or Poland last year, or Manchester ten years ago. It's very exciting.

Mother

"Sanskrit *matra*, like the Greek *meter*, meant both 'mother' and 'measurement'. Mathematics is, by derivation, 'mother-wisdom'. Root words for motherhood produced many words for calculation: metric, menstruation, mark, mentality: geo-metry, trigono-metry, etc. Women did temporal and spatial calculations for so long, that ... men once thought women were able to give birth because they had superior skill in measuring and figuring. Men imagined that if they could master these feminine skills, they could give birth, too." (Barbara G Walker, quoting from *Hindu Myths* by Wendy Doniger O'Flaherty in *The Woman's Encyclopedia of Myths and Secrets*, 1983)

The Oxford Dictionary of Etymology gives no indication of this theory, merely tracing *mother*, which, when it first entered English in the mid-C11th denoted a female parent, back to Old English *modor*, meaning womb.

For every definition of *mother* or a mother-combination term which contains connotations of love, respect and reverence there seems to be another connoting fear, hatred or disrespect.

One such definition is *Mother Nature* (since 1601); the mother in this sense is represented as both good and bad - a protecting and a controlling power - of which Dorothy Dinnerstein writes: "The mother, then - like nature, which sends blizzards and locusts as well as sunshine and strawberries - is perceived as capricious, sometimes actively malevolent."

Since 1000, *mother* has been applied figuratively to the protecting care exercised by a mother, or to the affectionate reverence due to a mother e.g. the Church, state, earth etc. On the other hand, motherly love and tenderness could be smothering: since 1880 a *mother's boy* has been a derogatory term to men.

The phrase *like mother makes it* (late C19th - C20th) means very well cooked and extremely tasty; but *mother's milk* and *mother's ruin* in the C19th denoted gin, with reference to the harmful effects of alcohol.

Respect is paid to one's *mother tongue* (since c1380), the first language learned as a child. The expression *mothers' meeting* has no connotation of respect as it is used facetiously to refer to a group of people, men as well as women, who meet to gossip.

Reprinted from Womanwords by Jane Mills (Published 1991 by Virago Press)

Charlotte Keatley adds

"The word "gossip" is derived from "god sister", the women who gathered round a new mother to give advice, practical support and hands on knowledge. What does it tell us about society that the word for this kind of meeting - "gossip" is used to mean idle chat? Most of the scenes in *My Mother Said I Never Should* could be defined as gossip. Why do you think there have been so few plays across the centuries in which we see women talking together?"

My mother said....

GRACE MITCHELL Doris

"Always wear clean underwear in case you get knocked down. Try to have clean ears and behind the ears, keeping hair tidy and clean. As I grew up in hard times, during the thirties and forties, my mother taught me how to make good, tasty meals with cheaper cuts of meat and vegetables."

JANE LOWE Margaret

"My mother said I should always try to keep the peace."

ROBYN MOORE Jackie

"Strangely most of the advice my mother gave me was related to sex... don't use tampons until you've lost your virginity... never be the first to telephone a boy or display any interest...don't sit next to a 'bloke' when alone with him - leave a healthy distance between you because when a man gets the urge, there is no stopping him (still waiting)... don't have sex until you are sure that it is love, because once a man has had his way he loses respect for you...

More usefully, my mother gave me a wealth of advice concerning the preparation of food. She gave me a creative outlet and sense of enjoyment and fulfilment when it comes to cooking, especially for others."

PAULINE LYNCH Rosie

"I have to admit I can't actually remember any advice my mother gave me. When I mentioned this lack of memory to her she said, 'See, I knew you never listened'. In my mind, the advice always seemed to come a little too late, as in 'Pauline, that was a really, really stupid thing to do!'

In all fairness to my mum, I should say that as I'm writing this she's shaking her head in disbelief that I could have forgotten so many pieces of good advice. She jogged my memory a little:

1. Maintain a positive mental attitude.

2. It's nice to be nice.

3. If you can't think of anything nice to say, don't say anything at all.

4. You will at some point need your Maths O Grade.

I try to remember the first 3, but I gave up on number 4 a long time ago. Sorry, mum."

My mother said I never should

SCENE LIST

Act One

1. THE WASTEGROUND, A PLACE WHERE GIRLS COME TO PLAY.
2. DORIS' HOUSE, CHEADLE HULME, MANCHESTER

Christmas 1940 and May 1961

3. THE WASTEGROUND
4. MARGARET'S GARDEN, RAYNES PARK, LONDON

May 1969

5. DORIS' GARDEN, CHEADLE HULME

May 1961

6. JACKIE'S FLAT, MOSS SIDE, MANCHESTER

early December 1971

7. DORIS' GARDEN, CHEADLE HULME

August 1951

8. THE WASTEGROUND
9. CHEADLE HULME/RAYNES PARK

early December 1971

10. MARGARET'S GARDEN, RAYNES PARK

September 1979

Act Two

DORIS' HOUSE, CHEADLE HULME

December 1982

Act Three

1. DORIS' BACKYARD, OLDHAM

early April 1987

2. MARGARET'S OFFICE, CROYDON

Four days later

3. THE WASTEGROUND
4. HOSPITAL, LONDON

Late May 1987

5. MARGARET'S GARDEN, RAYNES PARK

Next morning

6. THE WASTEGROUND
7. DORIS' BACKYARD, OLDHAM

September 1987

8. DORIS' MOTHER'S HOUSE

May 1923

Cast

MARGARET
Jane Lowe

ROSIE
Pauline Lynch

DORIS
Grace Mitchell

JACKIE
Robyn Moore

Director DOMINIC COOKE
Designer ROBERT INNES HOPKINS
Lighting Designer PAUL RUSSELL
Music Composer GARY YERSHON
Movement Direction LIZ RANKEN
Assistant Director LYNNE GAGLIANO
Production Manager KATRINA GILROY
Company Stage Manager SARAH NORTHCOTT
Deputy Stage Manager ANNABEL INGRAM
Assistant Stage Manager MIKE DRAPER
Wardrobe Supervisor ANGELA BUTTERFIELD
Sign Interpreter MAVIS RHODES

Charlotte Keatley's agent:
Rod Hall, A P Watt Limited
20 John Street
London WC1N 2DR

JANE LOWE Margaret

Jane has played many of the great roles for women, including the title role in *Saint Joan* and Viola in *Twelfth Night* (Palace Theatre, Watford); the title role in *Hedda Gabler* and *Lady Macbeth* (Liverpool Playhouse); the title role in *Candida* and Hesione Hushabye in *Heartbreak House* (Citizen's Theatre); Martha in *Who's Afraid of Virginia Woolf?*, a role which she has now played five times. In 1994, she appeared in *Medea* in the West End and on Broadway. Other tours include *Tristram Shandy* (Cambridge Theatre Company); *Waving for Monstrous Regiment* and *The Beaux Stratagem* (RSC). TV work includes *Hetty Wainthropp Investigates* and *Wokenwell*.

PAULINE LYNCH Rosie

Pauline was born in Glasgow. In 1995, she graduated from Rose Bruford College of Speech and Drama where roles included Maggie Morrison in *Men Should Weep* (ICA), Varya in *The Cherry Orchard* and Porter/Hecate in *Macbeth*. Theatre work includes Nick Ward's adaptation of *The Decameron* (Gate) and Kate in *Judy Upton's Bruises* (Cottier Theatre, Glasgow). TV includes *A Mug's Game* (BBC Scotland) and *Soldier Soldier* (Carlton). Film includes Lizzie in *Trainspotting*.

GRACE MITCHELL Doris

Theatre includes: *Love on the Dole* (Oldham Coliseum and tour); *Prisoner Cell Block H* (No1 tour); *Eligies for Angels, Punks and Raging Queens* (Drill Hall) and *Three Girls in Blue* (West Yorkshire Playhouse). Grace also appeared in Stephen Daldry's original production of *An Inspector Calls* at York Theatre Royal. Television includes *The Bill* and *Wycliffe III*. Grace has a daughter, Ruth, who is also an actress.

ROBYN MOORE Jackie

Robyn Moore trained at the Drama Centre while a single mother. This would not have been possible without the support of her mother. Theatre work includes David Freeman's *Faust and Morte d'Arthur* (Lyric Hammersmith); Laura in *The Glass Menagerie* (Cambridge Theatre Company); Fringe work includes the title roles in Checkov's *The Woman with a Dog* and Dic Edwards' *Wittgenstein's Daughter* and various roles in *The Weavers* (Gate). Films for television include Jim Goddard's *Reasonable Force* and Peter Hall's *She's Been Away*. TV includes *The Bureaucracy of Love, Executive Stress, Poirot, The Bill, Casualty, Resnick, Resort to Murder* and *Call Red*.

DOMINIC COOKE Director

Directing credits include *The Weavers, Hunting Scenes from Lower Bavaria* (Gate, Notting Hill), *Kiss of the Spiderwoman* (Bolton Octagon), *Of Mice And Men* (Nottingham Playhouse), *Autogeddon*, co-directed with Charlotte Keatley (Edinburgh Assembly Room - winner of Fringe First), *Marriage of Figaro* (tour - winner of Manchester Evening News Award). Rehearsed readings/workshops at Royal Court, RNT Studio and Tricycle. As assistant director for the RSC 1993-94: *All's Well That Ends Well, Taming of the Shrew, Travesties, As You Like It, Changeling*. Re-directed *An Ideal Husband* for Peter Hall (Old Vic).

LYNNE GAGLIANO Assistant Director

Trained at Central School of Speech & Drama, where work included *Antigone*, *Trojan Women*, *Dr Faustus*, *Skinning Peeling*; Directed: *Charlotte* (Duke of Cambridge, Czech tour); Assistant Director: *The Weavers* (Gate)

ROBERT INNES HOPKINS Designer

Trained at Nottingham Polytechnic and finalist in the 1991 Linbury Prize for Stage Design. Theatre includes *The Comedy of Errors* (RSC), *Happy End* (Nottingham Playhouse), *Miss Julie* (Young Vic), *Spell, Hunger* and *Imperfect Librarian* (Young Vic Studio), *A Doll's House* (New End Theatre), *Hunting Scenes from Lower Bavaria* and *The Weavers* (Gate). Dance includes for Yolande Snaith Theatredance 3 pieces: *Should Accidentally Fall* (BBC), *Swinger* (The Place/BBC) and *Diction* (The Place). Opera includes *Peter Grimes* (Mumford Theatre, Cambridge), *Eugene Onegin* (French Institute) and *Ghosts* (Riverside Studios) and ROH revival of *Die Meistersinger von Nurnberg* (Teatro Regio Torino).

CHARLOTTE KEATLEY Playwright

Charlotte Keatley was nominated Laurence Olivier Most Promising Newcomer to British Theatre 1990 for *My Mother Said I Never Should*, which has been translated into fifteen languages. Charlotte has written for theatre, television and radio, and teaches playwriting in colleges and universities around Britain. She was Visiting Fellow in English at Cambridge University 1988-9. As a director, Charlotte collaborated with Dominic Cooke on *Autogeddon*, winning a 1991 Edinburgh Fringe First.

LIZ RANKEN Movement Director

Performer: DV8, Gloria. Winner Place Portfolio Choreographic Award, Capital Award (Edinburgh). Movement Director: *For Shared Experience, Anna Karenina, Mill on the Floss, War and Peace*; For the RSC, *Phonecian Women* (D: Katy Mitchell), *Richard III* and *As You Like It* (D: Steven Pimlott); With Dominic Cooke, *Hunting Scenes from Lower Bavaria* (Gate).

PAUL RUSSELL Lighting Designer

Recent theatre: *Max Klapper, A Life in Pictures* (Electric Cinema, Portobello), *Buried Treasure* (Lyric), *The Eleventh Commandment* (Hampstead), *Clocks & Whistles, Serving It Up, One Flea Spare, Trainspotting, In the Heart of America, Democracy, The Chinese Wolf Waiting at the Water's Edge* (Bush Theatre); *Silver Face, The Boat Plays, The Great Highway, Madness in Valencia* (Gate); *Exquisite Sister* West Yorkshire Playhouse), *Not a Game for Boys* (Royal Court) and *Yiddish Trojan Woman* (Cockpit). Opera includes *Snatched by the Gods, Broken Strings* (Almeida); *Linda Di Chamonix, Rape of Lucretia* (Guildhall), *Cosi Fan Tutti* (Ealing).

GARY YERSHON Music

Gary has written scores of scores for the theatre. Recent work includes music for *Art* (Wyndham's Theatre), *The Weavers* (Gate) and *Peter Pan* at West Yorkshire Playhouse, where he has been composer-in-residence for 1996. He has composed for both the Royal National Theatre and the RSC, and returns in 1997 for the new production of *Hamlet*. Gary has composed often for BBC radio - most recently for *The Red Field* - and his TV work includes the music for a perennial cartoon favourite, *James the Cat*.

Oxford Stage Company Education

Oxford Stage Company aims to create theatre that is inspiring, challenging and accessible. Its award winning programme of education and associated events enjoys a national reputation, illuminating the content and form of the productions and to enable the audience to actively engage with the work. A diverse and innovative programme of introductions, workshops, residencies, teachers' inset days, open rehearsals and post show discussions, run by expert practitioners, directors and actors accompanies Oxford Stage Company productions. *Events around Love is a Drug, Twelfth Night, The Provoked Wife* and *Hamlet* reached more than 8,000 young people. The *Making the Future* tour of 1995 brought with it an unprecedented series of associated events to run alongside new plays from Europe written specially for a young audience.

...and Access

Oxford Stage Company aims to make its productions as accessible as possible. To achieve this, a diverse range of services has been developed to accompany *My Mother Said I Never Should*, including a cast list and synopsis, sign interpreted performances for deaf and hard of hearing people, and audio-described performances for visually impaired people. There are programmes on audio cassette and both cast lists and synopses are available in large print and braille.

Mavis Rhodes will be sign interpreting performances of *My Mother Said I Never Should*. Born in Leeds to deaf parents, Mavis has used British Sign Language all her life. She regularly sign interprets at the West Yorkshire Playhouse.

Sign Interpreted Performances:
Lawrence Batley Theatre, Huddersfield (6 Feb)
The Oxford Playhouse (12 Feb)
Warwick Arts Centre, Coventry (6 Mar).

There will be Audio Introductions on cassette for visually impaired people at:
The Oxford Playhouse (12 Feb)
Warwick Arts Centre (6 Mar)
Liverpool Everyman (24 Apr).

OXFORD STAGE COMPANY

Oxford Stage Company is a leading national and international touring theatre company based in Oxford. Acclaimed for the energy, passion and vibrancy of each production, the Company offers a repertoire of Shakespeare, 20th century classics, devised work and new writing for young people. Oxford Stage Company aims to produce theatre that combines physical expressiveness with emotional truth, based on imagination and faithful response to the text. The Company believes that theatre is a living forum for the exploration of ideas, promoting fresh discussion of contemporary concerns.

Future Productions

SPRING 1997: Dario Fo's The Comic Mysteries (Mister Buffo) translated by Ed Emery
AUTUMN 1997: Shakespeare's sophisticated romantic comedy All's Well that Ends Well
SPRING 1998: Making the Future II - new plays for young people

Make your contribution to Oxford Stage Company's future

There are many ways of supporting Oxford Stage Company.

DONATIONS

The Gift Aid scheme allows Oxford Stage Company to reclaim basic rate income tax on donations of £400 or more. If you would like to make a regular donation, a Deed of Covenant enables Oxford Stage Company to reclaim back the tax that you have already paid on your gift. This increases its value by almost a third, at no extra cost to you.

LEGACIES

By making a charitable legacy in your Will, you can help ensure Oxford Stage Company's work continues into the future.

SPONSORSHIP

Oxford Stage Company is always pleased to discuss sponsorship possibilities. Packages can be tailored to your needs and may relate to any area of the Company's work. To discuss any of the above, please call Vanessa Stone, General Manager, on 01865 723238

OXFORD STAGE COMPANY

Oxford Stage Company is now Headlong Theatre. Visit www.headlongtheatre.co.uk for current information

15-19 George Street, Oxford OX1 2AU

Free mailing list 01865 245781
Education & Information Packs 01865 723238
Accessibility Services 01865 723238
Fax 01865 790625
Minicom 01865 204855

Introduction

Playwright has the same word ending as shipwright, wheelwright and cartwright; all ancient crafts. We are all makers of vehicles in which other people will make journeys. When I write a play I'm thinking in three dimensions, about the action, image, colour and sound. The words are the only part we can print, the record or map for constructing a live performance. Trying to assess a play from the page seems to me like trying to get the taste of a meal by reading the recipes. You have to read a play aloud, on its feet, to find out what the words mean.

In *My Mother Said I Never Should* the language is often a lie, or denial: women trying to be good, while the subtext bristles with anger and jealousy. One reason for having all-women protagonists in this play is that I could dramatize the way women use language and thus the way we construct a view of the world. Plays have mostly been written by and for men for two thousand years. Beckett, Pinter, Miller, Mamet, and many others have written about the twentieth century through male protagonists. It is only since the 1960s that women have begun to write plays in substantial numbers, and we often use female protagonists. However, theatre is an art form where male work is seen as universal, women's work an aberration from the norm. We don't read *Hamlet* as a play simply for neurotic young men: we read *Hamlet* as a metaphor for all humans. We need a great many more plays to be written by women so that female protagonists are seen as representative of society as well.

I wrote this play in 1985 when I was twenty-five. I had been making musical plays and performance art, as an actor, director and designer for about four years. I had watched about 250 plays a year in Britain and the Continent as a theatre critic – everything from Greek plays to Pina Bausch danstheater, Ibsen to Edinburgh fringe cabaret. Writing about how plays worked or didn't was a great education. I also learned about plays by acting, mostly waitresses, waifish daughters or disturbed children – the range of roles offered to small women without much bosom, like myself. Waiting offstage to say my two lines, I'd think about all the kinds of women I'd never seen in classic or contemporary plays; so I decided to write the kind of play I'd enjoy watching or acting in.

It's hard to say how long it takes to write a play. I wrote the first draft of *My Mother Said I Never Should* in about three weeks, and spent three years rewriting it. The kaleidoscopic time structure and the idea of seeing the characters as children as well as adults were there in the first draft. I wanted a structure that questions the story as it tells it. The child scenes are not childish, but a vision of the core of each one of us, later inhibited by the times we grow up in. I was trying to convert female experience into theatre, so I had to invent my own conventions.

It took me two readings and three productions before I felt satisfied with my job writing this play. I read everything aloud as I write, then try the script with actors to see if the text creates the images I want, listen to the questions of the director and finally sit with the audience to experience the play. I had a very important, supportive, intuitive relationship with the first director, Brigid Larmour, who directed the North West Playwrights Workshop

reading in 1986 and the premiere at Contact Theatre in 1987. I spent the
winter in between typing in a sleeping bag because my cottage was so cold,
and Brigid would turn up with take-outs and we'd analyse every line.
Subsequently the play was staged at the Royal Court in 1989, and I had a new
set of comments from the director of that production, Michael Attenborough.
I completely rewrote Act Two, added and subtracted other scenes. I made
some tiny but crucial changes after working on the Boston production in 1993
with director Charles Towers. Every word in the play published here has
earned its place as essential for the performance to work.

When I wrote *My Mother Said I Never Should* I was trying to work out what
kind of woman to be. This is not an autobiographical play – I write to explore
what I *don't* know, not what I know. I was aware that there are many more
choices available to women now than there were to our mothers, and their
mothers. So I split the century into four women through whom to explore the
massive new conflicts in family life and therefore in society. I was also aware
that our 'free' choices, as women or men, are in response to the lives of our
parents and grandparents, and the expectations of the society we grow up in.
I decided to dramatize this process. This play is political because the very
structure, as well as the content of each scene, examines how often we put up a
negative attitude to change.

This play has been performed far and wide but is often put in studios not
mainstages, (as happens to other plays by women) which suggests to me that
theatre tradition still sees women writing about family life as a small subject.
Actually, family rows and betrayals are the mainstay of our classics, from
Arthur Miller back to the oldest Greek dramas. The odd thing is we have
almost no portrayals of the mother-daughter relationship – even in the vast
and amazing range of Shakespeare, these are offstage. So I joined my four
characters as mother and daughter to put this powerful and dramatic bond of
love and jealousy at the centre of the play. Then I thought, let's see what
happens if you break the sacred taboo of motherhood, and one woman gives
away her child.

I had to clear the men offstage to show the power of female expectations:
women can be much more judgemental of each other than men. I wanted this
play to make women angry as well as nourish us. I wanted men to see this too,
because all the women in this play are involved with men, all their
expectations and choices are acting and reacting to the men around them. I
want theatre to make the audience talk on the way home; I write plays to ask
questions, not give answers.

Now I am married, and I have a daughter, born in May 1996, so I see and
react to this play differently, just as each person who sees it has a response
based on what is happening in their own lives. For all that I can describe what
I intended when I wrote this play, let me emphasise that for me, theatre is
most of all about going into the dark: to be enthralled, frightened and moved;
so there has to be a huge animal unconscious below and above the text,
shifting and surprising us each time we venture in to read, rehearse or watch
the play.

Charlotte Keatley, January 1997

My Mother Said I Never Should

My Mother Said I Never Should was premiered at the Contract
Theatre, Manchester, on 25 February 1987. The cast was as
follows:

Doris	Joan Campion
Margaret	Jenny Howe
Jackie	Jane Paton
Rosie	Michele Wade

Director Brigid Larmour
Designer Nettie Edwards

A revised version had its premiere at the Royal Court
Theatre, London, on 23 February 1989. The cast was as
follows:

Doris	Elizabeth Bradley
Margaret	Sheila Reid
Jackie	Jane Gurnett
Rosie	Shirley Henderson

Director Michael Attenborough
Designer Tanya McCallin

Characters

Doris Partington
Born: Oldham, February 1900. Engaged 1923, married Jack Bradley in Oldham, 1924. (Age 5 in child scenes, as in 1905)

Margaret Bradley
Born: Cheadle Hulme, April 1931. Married Ken Metcalfe in London, 1951. (Age 9 in child scenes, as in 1940)

Jackie Metcalfe
Born: London, July 1952. (Age 9 in child scenes, as in 1961)

Rosie Metcalfe
Born: Mosside, Manchester, September 1971. (Age 8 in child scenes, as in 1979)

The action takes place in Manchester, Oldham and London.

The setting should not be naturalistic. The ideal design is an empty space although the piano can effectively remain on stage throughout Acts One and Two. There are no sofas or furniture in this play. The setting should simply be a magic place where the characters can make contact with the earth.

In the child scenes, each girl is dressed contemporary to her own generation, in the clothes each wears as a child in the 'real' time scenes, e.g. Margaret wears her Christmas frock, Jackie wears her 1961 summer dress. There are no cute, little girls in this play. The children are fearsome and courageous (as children are) and to depict them otherwise in the play or on posters is to misrepresent the adults of whom they are the core.

There is an interval between Act Two and Act Three.

The solution to the Solitaire game is shown at the end of the play.

Act One

Scene One

The Wasteground, a place where girls come to play.

Enter four girls, each dressed contemporary to her own generation, singing:

My Mother said I never should,
Play with the gypsies in the wood,
If I did, she would say,
Naughty girl to disobey!

Rosie (*chanting*)   What are little girls made of? (*Coaxing* **Doris** *to answer.*) Ssh . . .

Doris   Sugar – and – (*Effort.*) – spice . . . ?

Margaret   And . . .

Doris (*hesitantly*)   And?

Margaret   All Things Nice.

Doris *squirming, doesn't want to repeat it.*

Jackie (*can't bear it any longer*)   Let's kill our Mummy.

Margaret   Whose Mummy?

Doris   Whose Mam? (*Copying.*)

Rosie   Yes, whose Mum?

Jackie   All our Mummies if you like?

Rosie   Who's going to do it?

Margaret (*to* **Jackie**)   Dare you!

Doris   . . . Dare you . . .

Jackie   We'll all do it.

Margaret   It's my tea-time . . .

Rosie   How?

Jackie   I dunno . . . Boiling oil.

Doris   . . . Dare you . . . (*Repeating*.)

Margaret   Shut up, baby.

Jackie   Tell you what –

Rosie   What –

Jackie   I've got a penknife. I've been keeping it for something special.

Rosie   You pinched it off Jimmy Tucker!

Jackie   And we'll get some string, and take Mummy down by the railway line where there's a hole in the fence, and I think you have to put a stake through her heart.

Rosie   We couldn't do them *all*. (*Pause*.) We haven't got enough string.

Jackie   Just ours, then. (*Conspiratorial*.) They're not in our gang. Also they don't count because they're babies. They can do their own Mummies when they're old enough.

Margaret   Do mine! – I don't like blood . . .

Jackie   Lucy Parker cut her finger off at school.

Margaret   I'll be sick.

Jackie   Only the top bit. (*Pause*.) Like a flap.

Doris   . . . Flip flap flop . . .

Rosie (*bends to* **Doris**)   Do you want us to do your Mum?

Margaret   She's too young to know.

Jackie   She's got no Daddy: if we do her Mummy, she'll be an orphan and then we'll be responsible.

Margaret   Her Mummy's all right – She gave us lemonade. (*Pause*.)

Rosie   . . . She'll split on us though. Then we'll be outlaws.

Jackie   Go away, baby.

Doris *cries*.

Jackie Go on. Go home. (*Pushes **Doris** away*.) Tea? Tea-time.

All Tea-time. Tea-time.

Doris *goes*.

Jackie Piggy.

Margaret She'd only cry when she saw the blood. Me, I'm not having any babies.

Rosie How d'you know?

Margaret I'm not getting married.

Rosie (*pause. Thinks*)   Well it still might grow.

Margaret What?

Rosie The seed. The baby seed, inside you.

Margaret It can't! Can it?

Jackie *has been arranging sweet wrappers*.

Rosie What are you doing?

Jackie Voodoo. We need bits of her finger-nail and hair and stuff.

Rosie . . . She might haunt us . . .

Jackie You don't know *anything*, do you.

Rosie *is subdued*. **Margaret** *comes to look*.

Margaret What's that for?

Rosie Voodoo, you wally.

Jackie We're going to have a séance. To call up . . . spirits from beyond the grave.

Margaret We do that at school.

Jackie Do you?

Margaret On Fridays. Take buttercups apart, and count their . . . sta – stay – . . . bits.

Jackie Shh! Hold hands. (*They obey*.) You have to repeat after me.

Margaret }
Rosie }   After me.

Lights dim a bit.

Jackie (*deepens voice*)   We call up the spirit of – Granny!

Rosie }
Margaret }   We call up the spirit of Granny!

Jackie   Who died three years ago last Wednesday. And lived in Twickenham. Amen.

Margaret }
Rosie }   Amen.

Lights darken.

Margaret   . . . It's getting dark . . .

Rosie   . . . What happens now? . . .

Jackie (*deep voice*)   YOU from beyond the grave! Tell us how to kill Mummy!

Lights almost blackout. Silence.

Jackie   YOU from beyond the grave, tell us –

Margaret *and* **Rosie** *see something, scream and run off.*

Figure of **Doris** *now as Gran appears upstage, walking slowly towards them.*

Jackie   Mummy! Mummy! (*Runs off after the others.*)

Doris *continues to walk forward, oblivious of above. She removes a dustsheet of World War Two blackout material from a large object which it has been completely covering. It is a baby grand piano.*
Margaret *is crouching underneath it, hidden from* **Doris** *by a pile of bedding also under the piano.* **Doris** *begins to dust the piano as the lights rise for Scene Two and the wireless begins to play.*

Scene Two

Cheadle Hulme, Christmas 1940. **Doris** *is 40.* **Margaret** *is 9. The sense of a large front room, with austere decor. No Christmas* *decorations except for a vase of white, wax Christmas roses with a red bow, on the baby grand piano.*

Doris *dusts the piano lovingly. The wireless plays George Formby's 'Chinese Laundry Blues'. A pile of bedding is folded under the piano.*

Doris (*singing along*)   'Oh Mr Wu, he's got a naughty eye that flickers, you ought to see it wobble when he's ironing ladies' –

Margaret   Knickers.

Doris   Margaret? Margaret! Where – (*Goes to the wireless and switches it off.*) – Come out!

Margaret (*from the bedding under the piano, with a doll in her hands*)   WHO was that?

Doris   I have to listen to the wireless. In case Mr Churchill makes an announcement. It is my duty.

Margaret   Knickers.

Doris   Margaret. Come Out!

Margaret   It was Suky.

Doris *walks around the piano.*

Margaret (*sings, at first softly*)   Suky take it off again, off again, off again, SUKY TAKE IT OFF AGAIN –

Doris (*pulls her out from under piano by her arm*)   Never, never!

Margaret   Suky! (*Comforts the doll.*)

Doris   I've told you before!

Margaret   You've hurt Suky's arm! Torn her dress!

Doris (*shakes her*)   *Will* you listen!

Margaret (*to the doll*)   Suky don't cry. Mummy will cuddle you.

Doris   I shall have to tell Father.

Margaret (*pause*)   . . . Sorry.

Doris   Pardon?

Margaret   I'm very sorry Mummy.

Doris   Mother.

Margaret (*pause*)   Mother.

Doris   And you've spoiled your frock. I'd just pressed that.

Margaret   Haven't! . . . Yes I have.

Doris   Have you done your practice?

Margaret (*trying a lie*)   Yes. Bits of Chopin and Ten Very Easy Carols.

Doris *removes carol music from piano and replaces it with a piece of Beethoven music.*

Doris   You ought to be on Beethoven now, not nursery rhymes. The amount we're paying for your tuition.

Margaret   You're not throwing them away?!

Doris   Of course not. They'll go to St Mark's Jumble. Let me hear Beethoven's Minuet in G, Margaret. Have you washed your hands?

Margaret *holds out her hands, palms up and then palms down.*

Doris   Good girl.

Margaret *sits down at the piano and starts to play, very shakily, Beethoven's Minuet in G. She sways from side to side.*

Doris   What on earth are you doing, Margaret?

Margaret   I'm swaying with passion. Like the fat lady in the Hallé Orchestra.

Doris   We'll have less passion and more perseverance, please.

Margaret *resumes playing. Sound of an air raid siren, distant. She plays on.* **Doris** *nods to emphasise the tempo.* **Margaret** *is still playing, but stumbling. Eventually:*

Doris   That will do nicely for this evening, Margaret. I think we shall get under the piano, now. Close the lid.

Margaret   Next Door have got a proper Anderson shelter.

Doris (*miffed*)   So shall we, presently. Father's been to the Depot but they've run out, had a pre-Christmas rush.

They arrange blankets, a quilt, a stone hot water bottle and a bolster. **Margaret** *hangs her Christmas stocking on the piano.*

Help Mother make the bed.

Margaret   Watch out Suky, here comes a big fat bomb! Wheee! Eeee – oww –d–d–d–d–

Doris   Margaret!

Margaret   Well it looks like a bomb.

Doris   It's a bolster.

Margaret   I *know*, I – Suky thinks –

Distant rumble of aeroplanes which continues through the rest of the scene.

S . . . Suky wants a Christmas stocking too. She's not very . . . brave.

Doris   Put your nightdress on.

Margaret   Where's my gas mask?

Doris   Here, see I'll put it by the bolster.

Margaret   Where will you and Father sleep?

Doris   In the hall.

Margaret   Why?

Doris   I think the ground floor is safest.

Margaret   Why?

Doris (*pause*)   Sometimes the bombs make the houses shake a little. They make holes in the roof. Nothing will fall on you there.

Margaret   Except the piano. (*Pause. Quietly.*) Gillian's Mother and Father sleep in one bed, not two.

Doris   Are you getting into bed? (*Rhetorical:* **Margaret** *isn't.*)

Margaret   Yes. (*Lights fade from here on.* **Margaret** *gets into bed.*) Suky − ! (*She holds the doll tight.*)

Doris   Tuck you up . . . tuck you in.

Margaret   Will Father Christmas know I'm under the piano?

Doris   I expect so − see Margaret, you're a parcel and I'm wrapping you up!

Margaret   *And* they've got a Christmas tree. Why can't *we* have a tree with candles? Can't we?

Doris   *Mayn't* we.

Margaret   Mayn't we.

Doris   No. Pine needles cause a mess. Besides, candles are dangerous.

Margaret   Can Hitler see them?

Doris   You never know.

Margaret (*impressed*)   Does Hitler fly over our house?

Doris   Have you said your prayers? (*Lights very dim now.*)

Margaret   No.

Doris   I'll say night-night then. (*Going.*)

Margaret   Stay a minute! (**Doris** *pauses.* **Margaret** *doesn't know how to keep her.*) Do you and Father say your prayers? (*Pause.*) Do you?

Doris   Father does. I think that does very nicely for the both of us.

Margaret   Do *you*?

Doris   I'm saying good night now.

Margaret   Will we win the war?

Doris   Not if you don't keep quiet and go to sleep. (**Doris** *goes to the door.*)

Margaret   What do you mean? (*Pause.*) Gillian says, in parts of Manchester there's nothing left, just bricks

squashed. She says people get squashed under there.
(*Silence.*) Mother? . . .

Doris   Father will be home soon.

Margaret (*calls*)   Mother – (*Pause.*) Mummy . . . (*Pause.*)
What happens when you die?

Doris (*long pause*)   I'll bring you some cocoa presently. (*She goes.*)

The sound of aircraft.

Margaret   Sssh Suky Ssh! – No, I won't hold you. You
ought to go to sleep now, by yourself. You don't need your
Mummy to kiss you. You're eight years old.

Lights black out. **Margaret** *exits taking the bedding with her.*
Jackie *takes her place under the piano.* **Doris** *returns, with a floral
overall over her clothes. Lights up bright. Birdsong. A May day, it is
1961.* **Doris** *is 61,* **Jackie** *is 9.*

Doris   Jackie? (*Peers under the piano.*) Jackie! What *are* you
doing under the piano?

Jackie   Seeing what it's like. Mummy says you used to put
her to bed under the piano here in the Second World War.
And listen to the wireless . . .

Doris   Margaret says you read a lot of books.

Jackie   Only 'cos she won't let me watch telly. Daddy does.
Why d'you call her Margaret?

Doris   Because she's *my* little girl. You are always your
Mother's child, my Mother used to say.

Jackie   She's my Mummy.

Doris   I'm her Mummy.

Jackie   Yes but she calls you 'Mother'. That's different.

Doris   How?

Jackie   Just is. (*Pause.*) You won't tell Mummy about the
cup I broke?

Doris   It was only utility.

Jackie   What's that?

Doris   From the war. (*Pause.*) I'll tell her . . . you've been a very good girl. All by yourself too. (*Pause.*) We'll go in the garden and break two jam jars presently.

Jackie   Why?

Doris   Everything goes in threes. If you break one thing, more is sure to follow.

Jackie   Is that true?

Doris   So they say.

Jackie   Who's they? (*She strokes the piano.*) Why has your bath got feet? This is very old wood.

Doris   As old as your grandparents. It's the first thing we bought after we got married.

Jackie   Yes it is a bit old-fashioned.

Doris (*rubs wood*)   Classical.

Jackie (*strokes the white flowers in the vase on the piano*)   Are these plastic?

Doris   No! *Wax.*

Jackie   Can't you afford plastic?

Doris   I've had those *years.* Since your mother was a little girl.

Jackie   We've got new kitchen chairs with yellow seats.

Doris   Yes. Your Mother likes all these new formicas, doesn't she. (*Disapproving.*)

Jackie   When you spill your lunch you can wipe it off straight away. *All* our furniture's new. Poor old Gran. It's all old here, isn't it?

Doris   It was new once. (*Pause.* **Jackie** *contemplates this.*)

Jackie   Do you know something?

Doris   What?

Jackie   I like your old house.

Doris (*pleased*)   You tell your Mother.

Jackie   Why?

Doris   Do it for me.

Jackie (*musing*)   We don't have a larder you can hide in, either.

Doris   We'll make fairy cakes, then we can give Margaret tea when she arrives. (*Pause.*)

Jackie   Lucy Parker in my class can do the hoola hoop to a hundred.

Doris   And later on I'll teach you how to say grace, in French.

Jackie   What for?

Doris (*holds out her hand*)   Come along, let's go and find Mrs Beeton.

Jackie *hugs* **Doris**. **Doris** *hesitates for a second, then bends and embraces* **Jackie**.

Doris   Kiss your old Granny, then.

Jackie (*kisses* **Doris**. **Doris** *kisses* **Jackie**)   It's much nicer here.

They go off together.

Lights dim again. **Doris** *re-enters, without her overall, dressed as at the beginning of the scene.* **Margaret** *is not there, but the doll lies a little way from the piano.* **Doris** *carries a utility ware mug.*

Doris   Margaret? I brought you some cocoa. (*Sound of planes, distant.*) Margaret? Are you alseep? . . . Dear? (*Silence.*) Well then. You'll just have to drink it cold in the morning. (*She sees the doll and picks it up. Going.*) Can't waste good sugar and cocoa. (*Goes.*)

Scene Three

The Wasteground. A secret place which only girls can get to. Two cats wail like babies. **Rosie** *runs in. She finds the bits of sweet wrapper from the voodoo in Scene One. Arranges them in the pattern which* **Jackie** *used. Looks at them for a moment. Picks them up. Scatters the pieces, watches them fall.* **Doris** *runs in.*

Rosie   Mum's got the curse. (*Pause.*) Maybe we did it!

Doris (*pause*)   What curse?

Rosie   *The* curse.

Doris   Oh. Yes . . . How d'you know she's got it?

Rosie   You can tell.

Doris   How?

Rosie   Just can. Mum's been cross with me all morning.

Doris   Well?

Rosie   Well you'd be cross if you'd been cursed. (*Pause.*) Like in that story. She might turn into something.

Doris   Will she die?

Rosie   You have the curse until you're an old, old lady.

Doris   Then what?

Rosie   Then it stops. (*Pause.*) *Then* you die.

Doris   Did she prick her finger and bleed?

Rosie   Dunno. She might've, but I didn't see any blood.

Doris   Cross your heart she's got the curse?

Rosie   And hope to die. (*Lowers her voice, conspiratorial.*) We were in the ABC having buns. Mum said she was going to the Ladies. When she came back, she said, 'We'd better go quickly, I've got the curse.' (*Pause.*) So I went into the Ladies to have a look . . . and, sure enough, on the wall, there it was!

Doris (*frightened*)   What?

Rosie   The little heart-shaped drawing!!

Stunned silence.

Doris   Oooh . . .

Rosie   I thought she'd been looking different. Sort of oldish in her face.

They savour the moment. Then, fast.

Rosie }
Doris }   Doctors and nurses!

Doris   Bags be nurse!

Rosie   I'll be doctor. (*Pause.*) Who'll be patient?

Doris   All right. I'll be patient and you be doctor and then it's my turn.

Rosie   I've brought our kit.

Rosie *opens a plastic carrier with rattling objects inside it.* **Rosie** *takes out a large sanitary towel and fits it over her head, with the loops over her ears.*

Rosie   Good morning Mrs Bradley what seems to be the trouble can you take your knickers off please.

Doris   I don't think we ought.

Rosie   You been telling?

Doris (*pause*)   No.

Rosie   You have.

Doris   I think Mam knows. What we do . . .

Rosie   How, dummy?

Doris (*pause*)   She says she can see inside my head.

Rosie   We'll just have to pretend, then. (*Coughs.*) Can you lie down please not very nice for the time of year is it.

Doris *hesitates, lies down.*

Rosie   Tut tut tut.

Doris   Is it very bad?

Rosie   I'll just have to feel it.

Doris (*jumps up*)   Don't touch.

Rosie   But you like it.

Doris   I might catch a babby.

Rosie   I think you've got one already.

Doris   That's my husband's fault, you can't trust him.

Rosie   How is your husband?

Doris   Oh he's upped and gone.

Rosie   Oh I am sorry.

Doris   I'm not. You must drop by for a cuppa. That's enough now, your turn.

They swap positions: **Doris** *wears the sanitary towel,* **Rosie** *lies down.*

Rosie   Will you have to stethoscope me?

Doris   Oh yes all right. (*Takes a kitchen funnel from the carrier bag and listens to* **Rosie***'s stomach.*)

Rosie   Can you hear anything?

Doris   Yes I think the babby's coming out.

Rosie   Shall I tell my husband?

Doris   No not yet. There's no cause for alarm.

Rosie   Will it hurt?

Doris   PUSH! It's like doing a big poo. Then the babby pops out.

Rosie   You know the yellow nightie we hid? Mum wore that when I was born. It's got a dark red stain on it.

Doris   It's not, it's brown.

Rosie   Blood dries up. When it's very old.

Doris   Truly? Let's go and look.

Rosie   When a baby's born they cut the cord.

Doris   What's that?

Rosie   It joins the baby to its mummy.

Doris (*contemplates*)   Let's be babbies tomorrow.

Rosie   No, it's weddings tomorrow.

Doris   Why?

Rosie   You have to get married first.

Scene Four

Raynes Park, London, May 1969. The garden of **Ken** *and*
Margaret'*s suburban semi.* **Jackie** *is nearly 18, wears flared jeans
with sewn-on badges;* **Margaret** *is 38, wears a flowered apron and
carries a tea towel.* **Jackie** *has her red transistor which blares the
Beatles' 'All You Need is Love'. She sprawls on the grass beside the
cherry tree, next to the swing.* **Margaret** *follows, flustered.*

Margaret (*switches off the transistor*)   I should never have let
you go to that party in Hammersmith!

Jackie   Please, Mummy, leave me alone.

Margaret   You said you were staying with his parents!

Jackie   We were. But they didn't mind us sleeping
together. Not everyone has your hang ups.

Margaret   Oh you can wound me sometimes, Jackie!

Jackie   You sound like Granny now.

Margaret   What am I going to tell Daddy?

Jackie   If you want me to behave like an adult, then stop
treating me like a child!

Margaret (*pause*)   You don't know what might happen.

Jackie   I might fall in love.

Margaret (*trying to ignore this*)   You can get pregnant the
first time, you know.

Jackie   Thanks for telling me now.

Margaret   Well if you'd come to me and said –

Jackie   Well I did say I wanted to have a talk with you, actually, and you said 'Tell me while we go round the garden centre', don't you remember? (*Slight pause.*) Anyway, you can't scare me, because I'm on the pill, OK?

Margaret   Since when?

Jackie   Since before Neil and I went away at half term. You knew that because you've been reading my diary.

Margaret (*momentarily caught*)   Well I've no idea, you might be on drugs, anything! (*Collects herself.*) I know I'm going to sound like an old fuddy duddy. . . . but . . . (*Stuck.*) It's a serious step you've taken, you've no idea –

Jackie   It was no big deal. It was a relief to get it over with. I cried afterwards. Then I laughed. I expect it's better with someone you're in love with.

Margaret   You could have waited.

Jackie   Why?

Margaret   I had to.

Jackie   That's it, isn't it? (*Gets up and goes to the house.*)

Margaret   If this affects your A levels!

Jackie (*stops*)   What?

Silence. **Margaret** *has nothing to say.*

Jackie   I'm going to make a phone call. Phone Neil. (*Goes into the house.*)

Margaret (*pause. Picks up* **Jackie**'*s transistor*)   I had an admirer. He took me to dinner. I'd never eaten oysters before. – Wouldn't let me see the bill, that sort of man. I was sure Ken could tell, when I got in. I'd had my hair done, on a Wednesday. (*Pause.*) Ten years ago.

Blackout.

Scene Five

Cheadle Hulme, Manchester, 1961 as in Scene Two. **Jackie** *is 9,* **Margaret** *is 30,* **Doris** *is 61. The garden. Sound of lawnmower off right.*

Doris *enters with a chair and a rug, and arranges them on the grass. She glares, off right.*

Doris (*calls to right*)   Jack! JACK!

The lawnmower sound stops.

Doris   Are you coming to have tea with us? Ken and Margaret can't stop long.

Pause. The lawnmower sound starts up again. She shouts.

Well you'd better do round the front, I don't want grass clippings in our tea. (*As the lawnmower fades away to right.*) And mind my lily of the valley! (*She goes back to the house for the tea tray.*)

Enter **Jackie** *leading* **Margaret** *by the hand, followed by* **Doris**.

Jackie   And I've been doing the pear tree. Look. (*She shows* **Margaret** *the painting.*)

Margaret   Oh that's lovely darling!

Jackie   Grandad let me use his real paints.

Doris   He's been teaching you, hasn't he.

Jackie   Did you know shadows are purple?

Doris   Have you said hello properly?

Jackie (*hugs* **Margaret**)   Are you better?

Margaret   Better? (*Looks at* **Doris**.) Mother . . .

Jackie   Where's Daddy?

Margaret   He's gone to fill up the car with petrol.

Doris   That chair's for you.

Margaret   No, really.

Doris   The rug will do quite nicely for me. (*Sits.*) Sit down and have some tea.

Margaret   Oh we mustn't, I said to Ken we'd be ready to leave as soon as he comes back.

Doris   Her bag is packed and in the hall.

Margaret   If we stay for tea we won't get home to London till way past Jackie's bedtime.

Jackie   I don't mind.

Doris   Jackie made the cakes. Didn't you dear?

Pause. **Margaret** *gives in to pressure and sits.*

Margaret   All right Mother. And what have you been doing, darling?

Jackie   I broke a cup and then we broke two jam jars.

Margaret   Oh dear.

Doris   Jackie's been an angel.

Jackie (*offering the cake*)   Have the yellow one with the smartie.

Doris   I hope you've been taking the iron tablets, dear.

Margaret (*resists temptation to answer back. To* **Jackie**, *for the cake*)   Thank you.

Jackie (*says grace in French, very fast*)   Que Dieu benisse nôtre pain quotidien. Amen. (*Pause.*)

Margaret   Well this is very nice.

Doris   And how was Windermere? Did you drive about much?

Margaret   We stayed in a lovely guest house, a bit pricey but Ken insisted I was pampered.

Jackie   What's pampered?

Doris   Nursed.

Pause. **Jackie** *looks at* **Margaret**. **Margaret** *looks at* **Doris**.

Margaret No, pampered is – being spoiled a bit – like you've been, here!

Doris Thank you, Margaret.

Margaret And I brought you some Kendal mint cake! (*Gives it to* **Jackie**.)

Jackie And some for Granny? Never mind Granny, we can share this. (*Breaks it in half and gives half to* **Doris**, *then goes back to her painting*.)

Doris I hope you didn't do too much walking.

Margaret It rained a lot. Luckily there was a nice lounge with a fire. Time to sit and think. You know, Mother, I thought I didn't want it, till I lost it. (*Pause*.) It's been a blessing, you taking Jackie for the week. But I missed you, darling!

Jackie (*goes and hugs* **Margaret**) I cried the first night, didn't I Granny, then at breakfast Grandad let me have your old napkin ring.

Margaret (*holds her*) Oh Jackie.

Jackie And your doll. It's like a real baby, it's got real curled up toes and fingers. I was practising. I bathed it and put it to sleep, and it shut its eyes.

Margaret No! (*Gets up*.)

Jackie Mummy –

Doris Jackie – (*Catches hold of her*.)

Jackie I didn't break her, I didn't break the doll!

Doris (*comforts*) Ssh ssh –

Jackie You're hurting! (*Breaks free and runs off, knocking the paint pot across the painting*.)

Doris If you hadn't been so hasty to get that temping job, you would never have lost the baby.

Margaret (*busying herself with the painting*). It'll dry in the evening sun, it'll be all right.

Doris　That's for Jack. He wanted something from his grandchild.

Doris *takes the painting.*

Blackout.

Scene Six

A council flat on the Hulme estate, Manchester, early December 1971. **Jackie** *is 19½,* **Rosie** *is 3 months,* **Margaret** *is 40. A worn piece of rusty red carpet with ashtrays and mugs strewn on it, also the red transistor from Scene Four, now worn and battered, blares out over* **Rosie***'s crying. A Moses basket of blankets represents* **Rosie***; the actress playing* **Rosie** *can be seen making the sounds of the baby crying. As the lights rise,* **Jackie** *is packing baby clothes into a holdall.*

Radio (*Manchester DJ*)　. . . Today's highest temperature is expected to be a cold 3°, so wrap up warm. Most roads in the city have been cleared now, but there's still ice and snow on the Pennines, and the forecast is more snow tonight. Police are asking motorists leaving Manchester on Northbound routes to drive slowly because of black ice. Meanwhile, here's something to remind you of summer days . . . (*Rolling Stones' 'Honky Tonk Woman'.*)

Jackie (*packing hurriedly*)　I wanted it to look nice and now it won't all go in!

Rosie *yells.*

Jackie (*hits transistor, which goes off*)　Ssh, Rosie, please –

Rosie *yells.*

Jackie　Shut up!

Rosie *stops crying abruptly.*

Jackie (*gently*)　Ssh, ssh, there now . . . Where do you get the energy from, yelling all night? (*Bends over Moses basket, sings haphazard tune.*) My little rabbit, in your little basket . . .

Rosie *coos.*

Jackie   Sleep, beautiful . . . ssh . . .

Rosie *makes a little cry as* **Jackie** *moves away to pack again.*

Jackie (*bends over* **Rosie** *again*)   Please don't be crying when Mummy and Daddy arrive! – Where's your red sock? (*Picks it up and dangles it over* **Rosie**, *who quietens during*:) Look, it fell out! Give me a smile – yes! There. I even washed your red sock. Washed everything, don't want Mummy to think – (*Holding back tears.*) I've got to clear up, Rosie. – All these ashtrays, Sandra and Hugh last night, they never think about you, do they? (*Picks up ashtray.*)

Margaret (*from off*)   Hello?

Jackie   Oh shit, the mess – Come in!

Margaret (*entering*)   Hello Jackie.

Jackie (*immediately casual*)   Hi Mummy.

Margaret   It's not locked!

Jackie   I knew it would be you.

Margaret   You've been smoking.

Jackie   Journey from London OK?

Margaret   Not how I remembered, Mosside. All these tower blocks . . .

Jackie   Is Daddy – he's not –

Margaret   Waiting in the car.

Jackie   He didn't mind? – I'm sorry, I couldn't face –

Margaret   He understands.

Pause.

Jackie   This is Rosie, Mummy.

Margaret   I – came up the stairs. (*Pause.*) Lift is out of order. (*Pause.*) Lot of stairs.

Jackie   . . . Please.

Margaret (*long pause*)   Three months.

Jackie   Say hello.

Margaret (*goes to the Moses basket. Pause*)   Pretty.

Jackie (*goes also*)   You think so?

Margaret   You had curly eyelashes like that.

Jackie (*pleased*)   Did I?

Margaret   Hello Rosie . . . (*Kisses her.*)

Jackie   Don't wake her!

Margaret   Of course not!

Jackie   I'm sorry, it's just –

Margaret   You think I don't know?

Rosie *coos quietly.*

Margaret (*very tenderly*)   Ssh, there now.

Rosie *murmurs.*

Jackie (*turns away*)   I've packed her things . . . here. (*Gives* **Margaret** *the holdall.*) And her bottles are in this carrier. There's a bit of powdered milk left –

Margaret   Oh you really don't need –

Jackie   Well what would I do with it?

Awkward pause. **Margaret** *looks through the clothes in the holdall.*

Margaret   I've been to Mothercare. Got some of those new disposable nappies, like you said. Quite different from when you were a baby. (*Sees another carrier, goes to pick it up.*) What about this bag – what a sweet – won't she want this dress with the rabbit on?

Jackie   Leave those! – Things she's grown out of.

Margaret   Why did you have to try! All by yourself? Didn't you believe me?

Jackie   I wanted to see if our theories worked . . . (*Pause.*) But when I came back from hospital everyone had cleared out. You'd think I had VD, not a new baby.

Margaret He should be here with you, your – (*Stuck for word.*) – Rosie's father. – You in these flats . . .

Jackie (*calm*) Mummy, I told you. He visits; and sends money. It was my decision.

Margaret Yes but you had no idea! I told you, I told you! Nothing, for nearly three months, nothing, since the day she was born, then a phone call, out of the blue, the potatoes boiled dry!

Jackie You knew I'd phone, one day. (*Slight pause.*)

Margaret Look at you now, a year ago you had everything, you were so excited about the art school, new friends, doing so well –

Jackie (*angry*) I'll go back! Yes I will, finish the degree, I won't fail both things! Only think about her at night, her cheek against mine, soft and furry, like an apricot . . .

Rosie *makes a snuffling noise in her sleep.*

Jackie . . . She'll be happy, won't she? . . .

Margaret After you phoned . . . after you asked us . . . Daddy went upstairs and got your old high chair down from the attic. (*Pause.*) Like sisters, he said. A new little sister . . . (*Bends down to* **Rosie**.) Aren't you, precious?

Jackie (*panics*) Mummy – she's got to know – I can't come and visit, with her not knowing, I can't!

Margaret Jackie, darling, we can't go over this again – you know as well as I do it would be impossible –

Jackie I don't believe you!

Margaret When she's grown up, you can tell her; when she's sixteen.

Jackie It'll be too late!

Silence.

Give me back the bags.

Margaret (*gently*) You've got such opportunities.

Jackie   Expectations.

Margaret   Yes!

Jackie   Yours.

Margaret   You've got to –

Jackie   Why? (*Pulls away holdall.*) Why not just Rosie?

Margaret   You've got to go further than me – and Rosie too. (*Quietly.*) Otherwise . . . what's it been worth?

Jackie (*pause*)   Here, take them. (*Gives* **Margaret** *the bags.*) You haven't told Granny and Grandad?

Margaret   Not yet. I'll talk to them. (*Tentative.*) – Perhaps you could stay with them, just till Christmas, while you find a new flat? . . . (*Bends to* **Rosie**.) My little lamb . . . What's this?

Jackie   She has to have a red sock to go to sleep.

Margaret   You keep one.

Jackie (*puts one sock in her pocket*)   Love her for me . . .

Margaret *picks up the Moses basket.*

Jackie   I'll help you to the car.

Margaret   It's all right, Daddy will be there. (**Margaret** *picks up the bags. As she goes to the door.*)

Jackie   I'll come for Christmas. And visit, lots. (*Pause.*) Whenever I can afford the fare to London.

Margaret *exits.*

Jackie (*calls after them*)   Sing to her at bathtime, especially the rabbit song . . . (*Silence. Pause. She picks up the bag she told* **Margaret** *to leave. As she pulls out the clothes, she is suddenly hysterically happy. She holds up the rabbit dress.*) – Wore this the day you first smiled, you wouldn't let go of my hair, – do you remember?! (*Holds up another.*) – And your first bonnet . . . (*Gentle.*) And the shawl . . . wrapped you up, like a parcel, the day we left hospital; all the way back in a taxi, bringing you home . . . (*Pause.*) Our secrets, Rosie. I'll take care of them. (*Pause*.) You'll never call me 'Mummy'. (*Silence. Screams*.) Rosie! Come back! – Mummy, Mummy!

Blackout. For a moment in the darkness, the sound of a baby crying. In a dim light we see **Margaret** *rocking a bundle. She comforts the baby with the following words, until the baby quietens and coos:*

Margaret   There now, there now, hush! Did you have a nasty dream? My precious. Mummy's here now. Mummy's here, Rosie. There now . . . Did you have a bad dream, Jackie? It's all right. Ssh . . . ssh . . .

As the lights come up bright for the next scene, **Margaret** *turns and billows out the sheet which was forming the bundle.*

Scene Seven

Cheadle Hulme, Manchester, 1951. A hot August day. A distant rumble of thunder. **Doris** *wearing a sensible beige skirt, and* **Margaret**, *wearing ski pants, are in the garden folding a single bed sheet. One more sheet remains on the line and one of* **Jack**'s *shirts. Socks lie on the grass, one maroon one a little way off. The rest of the washing is already folded and in a washing basket.* **Doris** *is 51 and* **Margaret** *is 20.*

Doris   I'll be glad when they put an end to clothes rationing. These sheets are quite threadbare in the middle.

Sound of light aircraft going overhead.

(*Studies the sky*.) RAF from the base at Padgate.

Margaret   They're B29s, not Lancasters!

Doris   I'll be glad when they're gone. (*Disdain*.) Americans.

Margaret   Mother! Without them we couldn't have won the –

Doris   Are you going to help me fold this sheet, or are you just going to stand there all afternoon identifying aircraft!

Margaret (*staring at the sky*)   Maybe one of them's Ken.

Doris (*they hold the sheet by the corners and tug*)   I don't see how it can be, if he's calling in half an hour.

They shake the sheet vigorously.

Margaret   I can't wait to live in London! (*No reply.*) Ken says he can get a job there. He's frightfully clever.

They balloon the sheet up into the air.

Margaret   I'm in love, Mother.

Distant rumble of thunder. **Doris** *looks up at the sky.*

Doris   It's not going to hold. (*Pause.*)

They pull diagonals to stretch the sheet.

Margaret   And I'm going to learn to type! Ken says it will be helpful if we need a second income. (*As they shake the sheet.*) Typing's far more useful than all those stupid school certificates. I'll get a *proper* job.

Doris   What do you call running a home? (*Looks up at the sky.*) I knew we were in for a storm.

Margaret   I'm not wasting my life.

Doris (*angry*)   Thank you Margaret! (*They fold the sheet lengthwise.*) Pull! (**Margaret** *pulls so hard that* **Doris** *lets go and they jerk back from each other.*)

Doris   There's no need to snatch it out of my hands! There see, now you've spoiled it all.

Margaret   Well you can pick it up again, can't you! (*Pause.* **Doris** *picks it up, they resume folding.*) I'm not going to have a family, babies and all that. Ken and I have decided.

Doris (*distant rumble of thunder*)   It will break, soon.

They fold the sheet lengthwise.

And what makes you so sure you can keep Mother Nature at bay?

They close in chest to chest and **Margaret** *gives her corners to* **Doris**, *who folds the sheet in half and half again during.*

Margaret (*grandly*) There's THINGS you can get . . .
I've heard about them.

Doris I'm not talking about that. (*Cradles folded sheet.*) I'm
talking about the *desire* . . . for little arms reaching up and
clinging round your neck. (*She buries her face in the sheet, then
holds it out to* **Margaret** *to do likewise.*) Smell: lavender. From
the beds, there. Mother Nature is very hard to fight. It's not
just a question of rubber things or what have you.

Margaret 'Little arms clinging' . . . There, see, that's
what I don't want. That's the difference between our
generations. Mother.

Doris Well I'm glad to know you've worked it out,
Margaret. Can you sort out Father's socks, please?

Margaret (*picking the socks off the grass and pairing them*) You
want a nice snapshot for the family album don't you? Proof,
to show the neighbours. Well I'm going to be different!
Women did so much during the war: there's nothing to stop
us now.

Doris Ha!

Margaret You think I'm being selfish, don't you?

Doris I felt a few drops, then. (*Pause.*) What makes you
think I wanted children?

Margaret Mother!

Doris I had a job once too. I know it was only teaching,
but . . . (*Pause. To stop herself.*) there's an odd maroon one
over there, on the grass. (*Pause. Warning* **Margaret**.) Of
course, Father has absolutely no idea. One would never . . .
tell him. (*Pause.*) There wasn't any choice, then; so I don't
know whether it was my need – to love him, if you know what
I mean . . . or his desire – for a son. (*Long pause.* **Doris** *bends
and picks up a sock.*) Horrible colours he likes. Not my choice,
maroon . . . Not my choice at all . . . (*Pause.*)

Margaret The garden is always so lovely, Mother. May I
take a cutting, off one of your geraniums, to London with
me?

Doris Oh Margaret . . . why does it have to be London? (*Sound of raucous car horn, which repeats.*) Oh I do wish people wouldn't do that! Brings down the tone of the neighbourhood!

Margaret It's Ken! He's bought an Austin Healey – it's got a folding roof – you must come and see! I said to honk and I'd move Father's car into the garage so Ken can back into the drive – I'll have a lot of cases to load into the boot.

Doris That nice Graham next door. All those trips he took you on, to the ornamental gardens at Bellevue.

Margaret Yes, Mother. Well I'm *not* going to be a Manchester dentist's wife.

Doris I must say, Jack asked my mother before there was any talk of weddings.

Margaret Have you still got your posy?

Doris He's reversing straight into my lily of the valley!

Margaret He's not.

Doris He is.

Margaret He's not, just parking.

Doris Curious method of parking.

Margaret That's typical, you think all Americans are brash and wear loud check shirts and chew gum and want to marry English girls. You're just prej– . . .

Doris Margaret, that's enough! (*Pause.*) After all, he is going to marry an English girl.

Margaret Oh Mother, don't look at me like that with your lips pressed together.

Margaret *exits.*

Doris *folds the remaining sheet and puts it in the basket during this speech:*

Doris Well it's too late now. These sheets are damp. I knew this lovely summer wouldn't last. (*Pause.*) I suppose I should get the best service out, for tea. (*Rumble of thunder, close.*) She'll need bed linen. These are all worn out . . . Something old, something new. So they say.

Doris *picks up the basket of washing and starts towards the house. Crack of thunder overhead.* **Doris** *drops the basket, which spills everywhere. Immediately, the sound of pouring rain on leaves.* **Doris** *stands and contemplates the spoiled washing all around her as the pouring rain grows louder. Lights fade slowly to blackout.*

Scene Eight

The Wasteground. **Rosie** *skipping, chants.*

Rosie Georgie, Porgie pudding and pie,
Kiss the girls and make them cry,
When the girls come out to play –

Jackie (*runs up, one hand behind her back.* **Rosie** *stops.*) I went to the boys' den.

Rosie You said you wouldn't!

Jackie Only slightly.

Rosie You're out of the gang.

Jackie I got the penknife back.

Rosie I don't believe you.

Jackie (*takes the penknife from behind her back and holds it out between them*) So there.

Rosie So what.

Jackie I kissed a boy.

Rosie You didn't!

Jackie I did.

Rosie What's it like?

Jackie I think I'm in love.

Rosie How d'you know?

Jackie   Because this boy made me cry. Daddy makes Mummy cry and she says it's because she loves him. (*Opens penknife blade.*) Now we can do the Vow.

Rosie (*backing away*)   It's too late. You've probably got his seed now and it'll grow and grow and fill you up.

Jackie   You're still my best friend.

Rosie   Don't talk to me about best friends because I'm never playing with you again.

Jackie (*pause*)   Kissing wasn't as good as best friends.

Rosie   Why d'you do it then?

Jackie   To get the penknife.

Rosie (*pause*)   You didn't need to kiss a boy. You could have given him some bubble gum.

Jackie   I did. He wanted a kiss as well. (*Pause.* **Jackie** *holds the blade up.*) They said I'm a cissy.

Rosie   You are.

Jackie (*holds up index finger and ceremoniously jabs the tip with the penknife. Studies it*)   I'm bleeding.

Rosie   Do I do it too?

Jackie   Yes.

Rosie (*takes the knife and stabs her own index finger*)   Ready.

They face each other and hold fingertips together and recite.

Rosie }   Truth is honesty
Jackie }   Honesty is true,
            Keep your promise
            And I'll keep you.

They step back and suck their fingers, **Jackie** *puts the penknife away.*

Rosie   You can't ever lie to me now. (*Pause.*) Can you see into the future?

Jackie (*frightened*)   A bit.

Rosie   Will you have a look for me?

Jackie (*pause*)   It'll happen anyway. Mummy says don't cross bridges.

Rosie   Is that a spell?

Jackie   I don't know. She just says it.

Rosie   At night?

Jackie   I heard her say it to Daddy, in the garage.

Pause, they look at each other.

Rosie }
Jackie }   Don't cross-bridges!

Rosie   It must be a spell.

Blackout.

Scene Nine

Telephone conversation, early December 1971, later on the same day as Scene Six.

Margaret *in Raynes Park, London, aged 40.* **Doris** *in Cheadle Hulme, aged 71.* **Margaret** *dressed as for Scene Six, with the Moses basket beside her.*

Doris   Hello?

Margaret   Hello?

Doris   Margaret?

Margaret   Mother? Oh, I was just about to ring you. It's not gone six has it?

Doris   Two minutes ago. We've just got the news on.

Margaret   Oh dear . . . I'm sorry, I was just seeing to . . . (*Distant* **Rosie** *cries.*) . . . to Ken.

Doris   Is he poorly again?

Margaret   Oh, no, no! Well, a slight cold. Very slight.

Doris   *You* don't sound too well.

Margaret   I'm fine.

Doris   You don't look after yourself, dear.

Margaret (*pause*)   Mother, why did you ring?

Doris   Oh, just to see if you were all right . . .

Margaret   How did you know?

Doris (*matter of fact*)   What, dear?

At the same time **Rosie** *cries in the distance again.* **Margaret** *puts her hand over the receiver and collects herself.*

Margaret   How's Father?

Doris (*pause*)   We've still not seen Jackie.

Margaret   She's been . . . since when?

Doris   Well it's been a year, now.

Margaret   I've only seen her – slightly . . .

Doris   I suppose she's busy with her studies.

Margaret   Oh yes, very.

Doris   Only your Father and I thought she might visit, being in Manchester herself now. She's not moved?

Margaret   Well, yes, I'm not sure . . .

Doris   It was Jack's birthday last week.

Margaret   Didn't you get the cards?

Doris   Yes, very nice. (*Pause.*) But he usually gets a hand-painted one from Jackie.

Margaret   Well . . . you know how it is, she's got to rebel while she's still a teenager.

Doris   What?

Margaret   Revise. She's got to revise, for her exams.

Doris   We thought we might go and visit her.

Margaret   Oh no! I shouldn't . . . just yet. She's decorating, decorating her new flat.

Doris   She should have asked us. I've plenty of furnishings put by that I don't need any more.

Margaret   How's Father?

Doris   Oh, creeping, creeping. Can't do anything with his hands now of course. A mither [*pronounced my-ther*] he was in, trying to sign the will.

Margaret   You said.

Doris   So I sold his painting things. Some of those easels he's had since we were first married.

Margaret   Mother! Why didn't you tell me? Not the sable brushes?

Doris (*pause*)   No. Jack wants Jackie to have them. (*Pause.*) Of course I said to him I don't suppose she'll want those, being at a polytechnic. (*Pause.*) He sets great store by her, you know.

Margaret   I'd like you to come and visit us.

Doris   We're coming at Christmas. Or don't you want us this year?

Margaret   Of course Mother! I thought perhaps the week after next . . .

Doris   What is it?

Margaret   I can't explain on the phone.

Doris   You're not hiding anything from us?

Margaret   No!

Doris   Good or bad dear?

Margaret   What? Oh. (*Long pause.*) Good. (**Rosie** *cries, distant.*) Very.

Doris   It's not that sofa you were telling us about?

Margaret   No, it's . . .

Doris   Well that's two minutes dear. I'll finish now.

Margaret   Yes.

Father will be so pleased to know . . .

Margaret   What?

About Jackie.

Margaret   What?!

Doris   Revising for her exams. I'm saying good night now.

Margaret   Good night. (*The line has already gone dead.*)
Jackie, what are you doing to me . . . ?

Blackout on **Margaret** *and* **Doris**.

Scene Ten

Raynes Park, London, September 1979. The garden of **Ken** *and*
Margaret's *home. Distant jingle of ice-cream van.* **Rosie** *is 8.*
Jackie *is 27,* **Margaret** *is 48. The cherry tree has grown, the swing
is as in Scene Four. It is* **Rosie**'s *eighth birthday. Enter* **Rosie**,
carrying an old spoon and **Margaret**'s *doll Suky from Scene Two. It
is a baby doll, now bald except for a few tufts which have been spiked.*

Rosie   It's my birthday today and it's all gone wrong
already. I'm going to bury you, Suky. Eight is too old for
dolls. I want a Sex Pistols T-shirt. Some hope. Unless Jackie
brings me one! I'd have buried you ages and ages ago, Suky,
if you hadn't been Mum's. I couldn't care less now if Mum
sees me doing this. (*Digs in the tub.*) Suky. Stupid name. Even
cutting your hair off it won't go punk. I bet Mum cuddled
you and stuff, didn't she? Well I only hug people when I want
to, not when it's visitors. (*Holds doll over her face. Pause.*) When
I want to I can hug harder than anyone. In the world.
(*Pause.*) I'm saving it. (*Pause. Digs hole. Lowers the doll over it,
then holds it closer to her.*) I was going to give you away to the
Toy Collection at School, d'you know that? Mummies give
their babies away sometimes. They do. (*Pause. Slowly lays the
doll in the hole.*) Shut up crying. There, see, I'm putting you in
this urn. People get buried in urns. (*Covering the doll over with
earth.*) Jackie'll be here soon. She never cries. No one else at
school has a sister who's a grown-up. I might easily run away

with Jackie and live with her. Then you'd be sorry, Suky. So would Mum. (*Suddenly bright, as if enormously relieved.*) I'm going to paint the cherry tree now – for Jackie.

Rosie *lies on the grass painting.* **Jackie** *enters with a very lavish birthday cake and candles.*

Jackie   Happy-birthday-to-you! . . . Rosie?

Rosie   Why did you buy me one? Mum usually makes me one.

Jackie   Thanks.

Rosie   I mean, it doesn't look as good as this. And she always makes chocolate because she thinks I like it.

Jackie   Why don't you tell her you don't?

Rosie   Oh you know Mum. Never listens. I think she just likes making birthday cakes. Even *Dad* gets one!

Jackie   Let's light the candles.

Rosie   Shouldn't we wait for Mum?

Jackie   Oh, yes.

Rosie (*pause*)   Has it got drink in it?

Jackie   Rum. A bit.

Rosie   Mum and Dad never drink anything exciting. You know that funny shaped bottle you brought them from Mexico? It's still in the cabinet.

Jackie   Well I brought Mum some Greek lace this time. Sort of thing she wouldn't treat herself to.

Rosie   She's so *mean*! D'you know, she wouldn't even buy me a Sex Pistols T-shirt, she says 'No dear, you haven't grown out of last year's summer dresses.' As if I could be seen wearing those!

Margaret (*enters with a tray*)   What's that dear? Here we are, celebration drinks! How long is it since you were last here, Jackie?

Jackie (*silence*)   I don't know. Shall we light the candles Rosie?

Rosie   Can I?! (*As they light the candles.*) One . . . year . . . and four months.

Margaret   I thought we'd have some of the tequila you brought us, Jackie. We keep it for special occasions.

Jackie (*to* **Rosie**)   See.

Rosie   Me too?

Margaret   A little bit.

Pause. All three watch the candles burn.

Margaret   Magic.

Jackie   I used to wish . . .

Margaret (*cuts in*)   Blow the candles out.

Rosie   I think Jackie wants . . .

Margaret   Now darling, before it spoils.

A moment while **Rosie** *hesitates.*

Margaret   Blow the candles out.

Rosie (*blows the candles out*)   Done it! (*Pause.*)

Jackie   Wish, Rosie!

Margaret   No, you hold the knife and wish as you cut it . . .

Jackie   No, you wish *first*!

Margaret   No, Rosie and I always . . .

Rosie   Oh stop it, you two!

Margaret   Don't we, Rosie. (*Silence.*) *I'll* cut it then. It must have cost Jackie a lot.

Rosie   I don't want any now. (*Gets up.*)

Jackie   Don't go. What's this, Rosie love?

Rosie   You mustn't look! I can't paint like you can!

Jackie It's lovely, Rosie.

Rosie 'S not, the sun's running down into the grass.

Jackie It could be abstract, all swirls.

Rosie Don't be stupid! It's a mess, even you can see that.

Jackie Can I keep it?

Rosie (*snatches it away*) It's for Mum. Here, Mum. (*Gives it to her.*) It's gone wrong.

Margaret It's lovely! Thank you, pet. (*She and* **Rosie** *embrace.*) Say sorry to Jackie.

Rosie Sorry, Jackie.

Jackie *is watching intently.*

Margaret (*looks at the painting*) Where shall we put it? The kitchen walls are chock-a-block.

Rosie On the fridge.

Margaret (*laughs*) Run and put it there, before someone sits on it, like Daddy did.

Rosie *exits. Awkward pause.*

Margaret How's Manchester?

Jackie Fine.

Margaret Working hard?

Jackie Yes. (*Uneasy silence.*)

Margaret I've got a full-time job now, too.

Jackie (*pleased*) That's good. I'm hoping to open a gallery of my own in a couple of years, with Simon, if we can get the backing.

Margaret Oh I did like Simon.

Jackie We're not – together any more.

Margaret (*gently*) It would be nice, Jackie, if you found someone, I know you'll hate me for saying this, but it could be very lonely when you're –

Jackie Mummy – (*Stops.*) Simon wanted children, I tried to believe I could start again. – Stupid – I just kept dreaming about Rosie.

Moment.

Rosie (*calls*) Mum! – Where's the Blu-tac?

Margaret (*calls*) In the cupboard with the carrier bags.

Rosie (*calls*) Oh, s' all right . . .

Jackie She doesn't need me, does she?

Margaret No.

Rosie (*running in*) No what?

Jackie No you don't ride your bike on the main road.

Rosie I do! Me and Zoe Taylor nearly crashed, we were kazooming –

Jackie Well you shouldn't! NEVER, ever – I'm sorry Rosie, I didn't mean to shout at you – (**Rosie** *has run off. Silence.*) I do worry about her getting run over, or getting ill, or lost or attacked, and me not being there . . .

Margaret I worry about YOU.

Jackie Still?

Margaret Mothers don't grow out of it.

Jackie (*hands* **Margaret** *a small carefully wrapped package*) Here.

Margaret A present – for me? (*Opens it.*)

Jackie It's lace.

Margaret (*turning it over in her hands*) Where was it you were this time? – Greece? (*Bemused.*) I try to imagine what it's like, when you go off on these trips by yourself, no one else to think about!

Jackie It's from the convent on the island. The nuns have used the same pattern for a thousand years.

Margaret Thank you dear.

Jackie (*slight pause*)   Mummy, I've been given a rise; new bikes are expensive . . . I want to give you a cheque –

Margaret   How dare you! This isn't one of your art deals! (*Snatches the cheque and tears it up.*)

Rosie (*runs in*)   What is it Mum? (*Hugs* **Margaret**. *To* **Jackie**.) I hate you! (*Clings to* **Margaret**.) Mum, I want you to see where I've put my painting.

Margaret (*as they go into the house together*)   . . . All right darling.

Jackie *stays sitting a moment. She sees the old spoon and scattered earth, then goes to the cherry tree in its tub, digs out the doll which* **Rosie** *buried, brushes it down. It is naked except for one red sock.* **Jackie** *takes the other red sock from her pocket. As she puts the sock on the doll the lights fade to blackout, so that as she raises the doll to her cheek she is only just visible.*

Blackout.

Act Two

Cheadle Hulme, Manchester, December 1982. The large front room of **Doris** *and* **Jack***'s house. A French window to the garden and a door to the hall. Dustsheets over boxes and the piano. Snow on a rose bush outside the window.* **Doris** *is 82,* **Margaret** *is 51,* **Jackie** *is 30,* **Rosie** *is 11.*

Rosie (*enters with a flashlight, swings it round. Pause*)
Grandad? You in here? (*Silence, listens.*) Well if you're listening, I want to tell you that it was pretty stupid, what you did – I mean, leaving the house and stuff to Jackie. Mum and Gran were mega hurt, you know that? (*Pause.*)
Grandad . . . ? I'd like to know, did you do it because you like Jackie best . . . or because you're jealous? (*Silence. Listens. A rustle.* **Rosie** *jumps, swings the flashlight round.*) Mice. (*Pause.*)
I'm not scared of you, Grandad. it's the others who are. You didn't get me. (*Switches off the flashlight and goes out to garden through French windows, shutting them behind her.*)

Enter **Jackie** *carrying boxes and binliners. She puts these down and exits.*

Margaret *enters with a bag and rubber gloves, guiding* **Doris***.*

Doris   Two months ago Saturday Jack died, and the house hasn't been aired since.

Margaret   Well we can soon put that right, Mother.

Doris   I doubt it.

Lights on suddenly and bright. **Doris** *startled.*

Jackie (*re-enters*)   I turned the power on, and the water.

Doris   Oh I don't think that'll be necessary.

Margaret   Mother we have to see to clear up.

Jackie   You don't have to worry about bills now, Granny, I've worked it all out. (*To* **Margaret***.*) I've backed the van up the drive so we can load things straight in.

Doris   My lily of the valley!

Jackie   I couldn't see. There's snow over everything.

Doris   It was terrible on the motorway driving up.

Jackie   Have you had a good time in London?

Doris   . . . Terrible . . . (*Still referring to the journey.*)

Margaret   Yes well we're here now, Mother. Have some tea, I've brought a flask. (*Gets out the thermos and pours a cup.*)

Doris   I'm quite all right. You have some.

Margaret   I want to get on.

Jackie   Sit down while the house warms up.

Doris   I don't want to be a nuisance to anyone.

Margaret (*wavers, cup in hand*)   Jackie?

Jackie   Got sugar in it?

Margaret   Yes.

Jackie   You know I don't.

Margaret   You've got no sense of compromise, have you?

Rosie *knocks on the French windows with a white rose.*

Margaret   Look at Rosie.

Doris   She'll catch her death.

Margaret   She never does. (*Lets* **Rosie** *in.*)

Rosie   Look what I found!

Doris   Is it wax?

Margaret   A Christmas rose.

Doris   It's dead.

Jackie   It's not, it's frozen.

Rosie   That's dead.

Jackie   We could unfreeze it.

Rosie   Even you can't organise roses to come alive.

Doris (*going to French windows*)   They should all have been pruned by now . . . all blown down by the storms.

Rosie   C'mon, we can't prune them now.

Doris   I don't want whoever buys this house to think Jack and I didn't know about roses.

Jackie   We can pay to have the garden done, before we sell.

Doris (*stiff*)   All that money, and Jack would never spend a penny of it.

Rosie   Mum, can Jackie and I make a snowman?

Margaret   Rosie we've only got today and tomorrow to get this house sorted out. I don't suppose Jackie wants us in her flat any longer than that.

Jackie   Mummy, you can stay as long as you like, you know that!

Margaret   You said you've even been using your bedroom to store paintings.

Jackie   That was before the exhibition. Anyway Rosie's room is always ready.

Rosie   Mum, can't I stay –

Margaret (*sharp*)   Rosie. (*Pause.*) Now Jackie, you tell us all where to start. Seeing as Father left you in charge of everything.

Jackie   Come on Mummy, that's only because I live in Manchester too. He knew I'd be on the spot to deal with the house.

Margaret   I suppose being born in this house doesn't count, Jackie. (*Beat.*)

Jackie (*passing a binliner to* **Doris**)   Granny, you take a binliner and –

Doris   She's going to put it all in dustbins!

Jackie   You choose which curtains you'd like from this room, the rest we'll leave for the auction.

Margaret I'll make a start on the crockery, then. (*Pulls dustsheet off a set of shelves. A willow pattern service is on the lower shelves, ornaments and framed photographs above.*)

Rosie OK don't talk to me.

Margaret Rosie, bring that box over and start scrunching up newspaper for packing.

Rosie (*kicking the box over to* **Margaret**) Do some chores instead.

Jackie I'm sure you'll want to keep the willow pattern, won't you Granny?

Doris Old. Cracked.

They wrap and pack the willow pattern during the following dialogue.

Margaret Mother, you sit tight and we'll pass you things to wrap.

Doris I shan't want any of this. Jackie's possessions now, according to the will.

Jackie Granny, you'll need things for the house in Oldham.

Doris It's not a house. It's an end terrace.

Rosie Come off it Gran, that's a bit mean. Jackie bought you exactly the house you wanted.

Margaret Rosie! Don't be rude.

Rosie Well I think you're both being rude to Jackie. She can't help what Grandad did.

Doris It seems that sixty years of housewifery counted for nothing, in Jack's eyes.

Margaret Your house has always been a gleaming example to us, Mother. Rosie, can you fetch some more newspaper please.

Doris Well Jackie didn't follow it, did she. (*Slight pause.*) Jack noticed *her* sort of work, because he was always asking how her painting exhibitions were going. And since Jackie didn't care to visit much, I had to make it up. And as you know, modern art was never my strong point.

Rosie   She hardly ever visits us, Gran.

Jackie   – I'm always there for your birthdays, Rosie.

Rosie   Most of them.

Jackie   I try –

Rosie   S'OK Jackie, you have to travel lots, and your work's the most important thing, isn't it. (*Pause.*)

Margaret   Funny how a job was never a good enough excuse for me. I think Father disapproved of it.

Rosie   But your job's only typing, Mum. (*Slight pause.*) Anyway, Jackie's different, she's got no kids. (*Pause. One mug left at the back of the shelf.*)

Rosie   What's this vile mug?

Doris   That's utility, Rosie. I used to give Margaret cocoa in that.

Margaret   I'd forgotten.

Rosie   Mum's always giving us cocoa.

Margaret   It's funny, Mother, Jackie and Rosie don't even like cocoa.

Doris   You only want what you're denied.

Rosie *passes mug to* **Jackie**, *who wraps it.*

Jackie   Oh yes – I broke the handle once – see where Grandad glued it?

Margaret   I don't remember.

Jackie   Oh – you weren't here.

Margaret   Why ever not?

Jackie   Well it was the summer you – (*Stuck.*) – weren't well.

Margaret (*pause*)   I don't remember.

Pause. **Jackie** *puts the mug in the box which is now full and tapes it closed.*

Jackie   There's the willow pattern, Granny.

Doris   That was my wedding. Was never the set I wanted.

Pause.

Jackie   Rosie, take Granny into the kitchen and see if there's any pans she'd like to take.

Doris   What about the bedrooms?

Margaret   What about them, Mother?

Doris   Well Rosie will need bed linen.

Rosie   What for?

Doris   You never know.

Rosie   I've got a duvet.

Margaret   Rosie.

Rosie   I have!

Jackie   Rosie, why don't you and Granny go upstairs and sort out some sheets.

Doris   Come along, princess.

Rosie   I'm not a princess. I'm a punk. – We could get in your old wardrobe, Gran.

Doris   Why, love?

Rosie   Play sardines. Brill. – Come on Gran.

As **Rosie** *leads* **Doris** *out of the room.*

Doris   I want to know, when did I stop being Granny, and turn into Gran?

Rosie   You like it.

Pause.

Jackie   I thought we might have a chat.

Margaret   We can while we finish these shelves, can't we.

Jackie *does not reply. She fetches the stepladder and puts it by the shelves.*

Jackie   How's work?

Margaret   Fine. How's yours?

Jackie   Oh – OK. (*Pause.*) I'll climb, and pass you things.

They work.

Margaret   I read an article at the hairdressers, about a girl who does silk-screen printing, in Sheffield. Rather like you.

Jackie   I don't do silk-screen printing. (*Pause. Passes a frame.*) What a serious child you were!

Margaret (*looks at it*)   On the beach at Scarborough. I was six years old. I remember Father wanted a nice one . . .

Jackie   'The highest standard', he'd always say to me.

Margaret   1937. I remember Father kissing me that day, and saying, 'You're nearly grown up now.' He didn't kiss me after that. (*Pause.*) If you left a bit of butter on your plate, it was either Mother on at you about rationing, or Father would tell us again, how he started his business with a tin of boot polish, cleaning gentlemen's shoes on the steps of the Royal Exchange. What that had to do with butter, I really don't know.

Jackie (*lifts down a silver rose bowl*)   The rose bowl. 'Manchester Business Award, 1949'.

Margaret   He took me to the Exchange once, to look at his shares. Young women had to wait outside, of course. (*She has a spasm of pain.*)

Jackie   Mummy – is it upsetting you? – Sit down for a bit.

Margaret (*fighting pain*)   So much to do. (*Continues packing.*)

Jackie *looks worried.*

Margaret   Next shelf, Jackie.

Jackie   The pottery duck I made – look.

Margaret   Rosie made that.

Jackie No, I made it for Grandad.

Margaret I think I should know.

Jackie Mummy I –

Margaret *has another spasm of pain.*

Jackie Please stop doing things for a moment.

Margaret It's just menopause. Cramps . . . (*She sits.*)

Jackie It shouldn't do that to you. Have you seen a doctor?

Margaret Surgery hours are nine till six. I'm working then.

Pause.

Jackie Rosie's very energetic . . .

Margaret She's like you.

Jackie . . . I meant it Mummy, about school holidays.

Margaret And how would you cope, the hours you work?

Jackie (*pause*) I could time-share with Sandra at the City Art Gallery. I asked her. – She's got two small children now.

Pause.

Margaret All Rosie's schoolfriends are in London.

Pause.

Jackie It was just an offer. (*Clumsily.*) If you ever feel you can't cope –

Margaret What are you suggesting?!

Jackie Mummy, I want to ask you – (*Stops.*)

Margaret (*pause*) What?

They look at each other. Long pause.

Jackie Let's get on.

Margaret *gets up,* **Jackie** *climbs stepladder.*

Jackie When I've sold this house and invested the money for everyone, you won't have to work so hard.

Margaret I have to work. There's always something. I don't have your attitude to the future, Jackie.

Jackie (*pause.* **Jackie** *at top shelf*) That's everything. – No, what's this? (*Lifts down an old chocolate box. Opens it.*) – Look, a Victorian photograph! The frame's made of shells . . .

Margaret (*pauses*) That's Mother's Mother.

Jackie (*excited*) Is it? Look at that stiff black dress – and the high collar.

Margaret Goitre. Women over thirty never showed their necks in those days. Swellings. Hormone problem. No proper medicine to control it.

Jackie Why hasn't Granny ever showed us this?

Margaret (*pause*) Jack didn't like it. (*Pause.*) Mother grew up in what she calls – reduced circumstances . . . Her mother wasn't married.

Jackie – *stunned*.

Margaret I found out in a letter once.

Jackie (*fury*) How could you?

Margaret What?

Jackie Never tell me!

Margaret It wouldn't have made any difference, Jackie.

Jackie You know it would! (*Angry tears.*) Mummy –

A moment. **Jackie** *can't speak. Suddenly* **Rosie** *bursts into the room with a sheet over her head.*

Rosie Whoo-oo-oo! I'm a ghost.

Jackie Oh – (*She drops the framed photo, which breaks.*) Look what you made me do!

Rosie Sorry.

Margaret What on earth are you doing Rosie? – Where's Mother?

Rosie We're folding sheets. The landing's a snow storm.

Margaret (*weary*) Oh dear. I'd better go and look. – Jackie, you pick up the pieces. (*She exits.*)

Rosie Never mind Jackie. (*Kisses her.*) Look. Gran's cut holes for eyes in this sheet. She's done one for herself too, that'll give Mum a fright.

Jackie (*laughs*) Oh Rosie . . .

Rosie What?

Jackie I don't know . . .

Rosie What's up?

Jackie *fights tears. After a moment.*

Jackie Rosie, you must understand – (*Slight pause.*) Mummy has – a lot to cope with.

Rosie Oh, she's been telling you about Dad, hasn't she.

Jackie What about Dad?

Rosie Don't sound so worried. Why d'you always think things are your fault, Jackie?

Jackie – Does Mum work late?

Rosie Yeah. She's doing some new computer course in the evenings.

Jackie Does Dad mind?

Rosie Yeah, Mum drives him spare. They have rows a lot.

Jackie (*anxious*) What about?

Rosie Oh I dunno, the washing or something. I just put my Walkman on.

Jackie Poor Mummy . . . why didn't she tell me about it?

Rosie Well she doesn't want you to know she's messed things up. – C'mon, help me rip this sheet.

Jackie   What for?

They rip the sheet in half.

Rosie   A banner. We're doing a Greenham protest outside the physics lab at school.

Jackie   Why?

Rosie   Secrecy kills. (*Pause.*) – Nuclear secrecy. (*Pause.*) You can make one too. (*Holds out half sheet,* **Jackie** *takes it, raises it.*)

Jackie (*like a child making a wish*)   'Sorry Mummy'.

Rosie (*pause*)   How old are you?

Jackie   Thirty. Why?

Rosie   You should stop that sort of thing now, or you never will. You should hear Mum's 'I'm sorry' voice on the phone to Gran.

Jackie   Don't you worry about what Mummy thinks?

Rosie   I worry about nuclear war, and not getting a job, and whether Mr Walsh the physics teacher fancies me. Mum doesn't understand.

Jackie   Fancy not worrying.

Rosie   He's old enough to be my Dad. Mega creepy. – You're old enough to be my Mum! (*Pause.*) I'm glad you're not.

Jackie   Why?

Rosie   Because it would be a mega-pain having to live up to you. Grandad used to go on and on about you, you know.

Jackie   He disapproved of me.

Rosie   He didn't.

Jackie   I'm not how he thinks a woman should be.

Rosie   That's what he liked! You are dumb.

Jackie (*amazed*)   It wasn't admiration you know, his will! It was revenge.

Rosie   How?

Jackie   I'd escaped. Families. – Nearly. He's made me responsible for all of you now.

Rosie (*pause*)   You are thick. He left you the money so you can open a gallery of your own.

Jackie (*as she takes this in*)   What would you do with the money Grandad left?

Rosie   I'd buy a baseball jacket instead of this yucky anorak Mum makes me wear. I wouldn't give it all to Mum and Gran, like you. I'd give some to Greenpeace. – C'mon, let's go in the garden and practise our banners.

Rosie *opens the French windows and runs out swirling the sheet like a flag.* **Jackie** *hesitates.* **Doris** *enters, carrying a half-filled binliner.*

Doris   There's some washing flapping in the garden.

Jackie   It's Rosie. She wants to change the world. (*Pulls French windows shut.*)

Doris   You used to be like that.

Jackie   Have I changed so much?

Doris (*watches* **Rosie**)   It was thick snow, that winter you came to stay. After Margaret had taken Rosie. – Not that you were in much of a state to enjoy Christmas.

Jackie   You've still got my letter?

Doris   Of course.

Jackie   – Rosie must have it the day she's sixteen.

Doris   Oh you make me so angry, Jackie! – You have to ask for what you want.

Jackie   Granny, I can't!

Doris   You can.

Jackie   But Mummy's got so much to – it's not a good time for her.

Doris   There's always an excuse. (*Pause.*) I never did ask for what I wanted. Resentment is a terrible thing, Jackie.

You don't want to be resenting somebody at the end of your life.

Jackie (*avoiding this*)   What's in the binliner?

Doris (*stiffly*)   The pale blue curtains from the bedroom.

Jackie   Oh good. Pale blue's your favourite, isn't it.

Doris   Jack chose all the colours in this house (*Slight pause.*) Very artistic, visitors used to say. (*Pause.*) Scarlet, I'll have in my new house (*Pause.*)

Enter **Margaret** *carrying a binliner. As she puts it down.*

Margaret   Everything in the binliner is for Oxfam.

Doris   Nothing ventured, Jackie.

Jackie   Mummy . . .

Margaret   Jackie, if you're not doing anything, there's the spare room to sort out.

Jackie   Yes, Mummy.

There is a rumbling noise beyond the hall.

Doris   I told you that boiler wasn't right, Margaret.

Margaret   Yes Mother. (*She exits.*)

Jackie (*picks up binliner with curtains which* **Doris** *brought in*)   Shall I put these curtains with the stuff for Oxfam, Granny?

Doris   There's something else in that bag, Jackie. Some things you left with me once.

Jackie   What?

Doris   The baby clothes.

Jackie (*pause – can't cope*)   I'd better go and see if everything's all right in the kitchen.

Doris   Are you going to give them away?

Jackie   No. – Thank you, for keeping them safe, Granny.

Jackie *exits.* **Doris** *opens the French windows.*

Doris   Rosie!

Rosie *comes in laughing and breathless, with the banner.*

Doris   It's a waste of time. The world's going to end soon, I saw it on the television.

Rosie   That's only the official view, you mustn't believe them . . . But it was scary when it blew up, wasn't it?

Margaret (*entering*)   What's blown up, Rosie dear?

Rosie   The world.

Margaret   Oh. That's all right. I thought it was something else.

Doris   What?

Margaret   Nothing, Mother.

Doris   We thought perhaps the kitchen ceiling had come down. Jackie went to have a look. She's so good at that sort of thing.

Margaret (*wearily*)   Yes Mother. (*Exits.*)

Doris   They work too hard.

Rosie   You shouldn't wind them up.

Doris   You should be helping them.

Rosie   They'd only say I was more trouble.

They smile.

Doris   I'll show you something. (*Pulls the dustsheet of the piano from Act One.*)

Rosie (*pause*)   It's the piano.

Doris   Don't you like it?

Rosie   We've got a synth at school.

Doris   I had a friend called Cynth.

Rosie   What's this? (*Picks up a plate on top of the piano.*)

Doris   It's a salver. Jack's employees gave it him on his retirement. It's only plate, of course.

Rosie (*sniffs*)   The silver smells funny. I hate old things.

Doris   You hate dead things, not old things, Rosie. (*Pause.*) So do I. (*Pause.*) I'm old.

Rosie   Hold this. So you can see your face in it. (**Doris** *holds the plate*.) Sit down on the piano stool. (**Doris** *does so*.)

Doris   What are you going to do?

Rosie   Aha. Close your eyes.

Rosie *stands behind her and puts her hands on* **Doris**'*s cheeks, gently pulling the skin back and taut.*

Rosie   Smooth the wrinkles away . . .

Doris   Nice warm hands, Rosie.

Rosie   Now open your eyes, Gran.

Doris   Oh! (*She studies her reflection.*)

Rosie   There, see. You're not old really. Only on the surface. (*A moment. Then* **Rosie** *lets go.*) My outside's the same as my inside. That's why when I talk Mum thinks I'm being rude.

Doris (*gets up, puts the salver in the box*)   When you're old . . . if you're rude . . . they just think your mind is going. (*Pause.*) They never understand that it's anger. (*Pause.*) Help me polish the piano.

Rosie   Do I have to?

Doris   There's some dusters and polish in Margaret's holdall.

Rosie (*passes them. Reads tin*)   'Bradley's beeswax.' With a picture of a bee. Here.

Doris   That's Jack's firm, of course. (*Tries, then.*) Can you unscrew it?

Rosie (*does so*)   What was your surname, Gran?

Doris   Partington. Here, you take this cloth, and do the legs.

Rosie *does.*

They polish the piano during the following.

Rosie   We're doing a project about you at school.

Doris   About me?

Rosie   Yeah, you're working-class Lancashire, aren't you?

Doris   Do I look like it?

Rosie   Yeah . . . (*As if from school book.*) 'Oldham families were all cotton or paper. Despite the decline in the manufacturing industries, community spirit remained strong.'

Doris (*reminiscing*)   You'd give a neighbour a bit of sugar, bit of soap, what they needed. When the King came, we scooped up the manure for the tomatoes. Pride costs nothing.

Rosie   That's what they said on the documentary we saw at school.

Doris   Did they now. You've missed a bit there, see. When Mother and I arrived in Jubilee Street, the landlady, a big woman, arms like beef, though she wore fancy hats, said 'I didn't know you had a babby.' 'You never asked,' said Mother. She did! And that was that.

Rosie   You didn't have a Dad?

Doris   No.

Rosie   Does Mum know?

Doris   No.

Rosie   Can it be our secret?

Doris   If you like, Rosie. Of course people gossiped, but the girl next door was illegitimate too, it was more common than they put on those documentaries. I was instilled. To get on. Work hard and you will rise like bread, my mother said – Are you polishing that, or just resting your arm? – No one's ever told me what to do. Of course by the time I met Jack the neighbourhood wasn't what it used to be. Wicked things even in Oldham. Well, there was the Depression. When

you've got no job you lose a sense of things. But we worked.
We moved up. To Cheadle Hulme! (*Pause.*) It was very –
(*Pause.*) – snob. When Jack's parents came visiting I used to
borrow the silver teapot from Next Door. Got in a fix one
day, because Next Door's in-laws popped by the same
afternoon. We had to pass it through the window, back and
forth. (*Pause.*) I never used bicarb, for my scones, just elbow.
(*Rubs.*) There now. We can see our faces in it. (*Pause. Both
admire it.*) It will fetch quite a bit, I fancy.

Rosie   You can sell pianos through the small-ads.

Doris   Jackie's organised an auction, hasn't she? Put these
cloths away, they're soiled now.

Rosie *opens* **Margaret**'s *binliner, thinking it's rubbish.*

Doris   That's not rubbish –

Rosie   Hey it's full of clothes! (*Tips the binliner all over the
floor. Picks some up.*) Cheesecloth and flares! Yuck. I didn't
know you were a hippy once, Gran.

Doris   Oh quite a – what's the word – 'swinger'.

Rosie   No kidding?

Doris   No. (*Pause.*) Those were Jackie's – she came to stay
with us once, left some things she didn't need any more.

Rosie   Aren't they revolting! My big sister in these! (*Pulls
out the ski pants* **Margaret** *wore in Act One, Scene Seven.*) Oh, can
I have these ski pants?

Doris   You can have what you like. Margaret obviously
doesn't care for any of them. Everything's throwaway now,
of course.

Rosie   But these are brill Gran! mega trendy!

Rosie *pulls ski pants over her tights and skirt.*

Doris   You don't want those slacks. There's a nice beige
skirt here, see love. (*Picks out skirt she wore in Act One, Scene
Seven.*) Margaret bought those . . . 'Pants' . . . (*Disdain.*)
They're American.

Rosie Are they real fifties?

Doris There's generations here, all mixed up, if you poke about. (*Rummages in binliner.*)

Margaret *re-enters and goes to her holdall.*

Margaret Don't say I didn't bring rubber gloves . . .

She pulls a pair from her holdall and puts them on during:

Rosie Mum, look! (*Silence.*) – D'you recognise them? (*Silence.*) Gee, ah simply must do mah nails! (**Rosie** *parades about.*) – Mum?

Margaret Rosie we haven't time for dressing-up games.

Doris I think they rather suit her, Margaret.

Rosie They're really sexy. I can't imagine you fitting into these, Mum! – Did she look nice in them, Gran?

Pause.

Margaret Did I Mother?

Pause.

Rosie Can't you remember that far back?

Doris You only remember what you want.

Margaret Rosie, clear up this mess. We're going as soon as Jackie's fixed the boiler. (*She exits.*)

Rosie I'm keeping these on for going home. Will you help me put my hair up, like they did?

Doris (*helps* **Rosie** *put her hair up*) A beehive? Sugar and water you need that.

Rosie (*delight*)   – Like a punk!

They are stuffing clothes back into the binliner.

(*Amused.*) – Shall I keep this hippy stuff to show Jackie?

Doris I wouldn't bother.

Rosie Why not? – Really embarrass her!

Doris Not all memories are pleasant. (*Beat.*)

Rosie   We should hide some clothes in the cellar, for someone to find in a hundred years . . .

Doris *ties the binliner shut.* **Rosie** *reaches for the other one.*

Rosie   What's in here?

Doris   – Oh, just some old curtains.

Rosie (*opens it*)   What sweet little baby clothes! (*Tips them all over the floor.*) – You're not looking, Gran!

Doris   Put those back in the bag, Rosie.

Rosie   I want this one with the little rabbits on.

Doris   No. That belongs to Jackie.

Rosie   I'll ask Jackie then.

Doris   I should have known . . .

Enter **Jackie**, *distracted.*

Jackie   Did I leave the stepladder in here?

She stops, seeing the baby clothes everywhere.

Rosie (*holds up rabbit dress*)   Look what I found!

Jackie (*pause*)   Not your rabbit dress.

Rosie   – Mine? Gran, you said this was Jackie's.

Doris   Did I? Well, you ask Jackie.

Rosie *looks at* **Jackie**.

Jackie (*slowly*)   I bought it for you, Rosie.

Margaret (*calls from the hall*)   Jackie!

Rosie *whips the rabbit dress behind her just as* **Margaret** *enters on the line.*

Margaret   Are you helping me or not?

She stops and takes in the scene.

Rosie   Guess what Mum, you'll never guess!

Margaret (*terror*)   What.

Rosie   GUESS!

(*She brings out the rabbit dress from behind her back.*) – My baby dress! (*Pause.*) And guess what Jackie told me –

Margaret (*giddy*)   No . . .

Jackie   It's OK everyone. Mummy it's OK.

She goes to **Margaret** *but they can't hold each other.*

Rosie   What?

Jackie   Mummy's . . . not feeling well. Are you?

Margaret   I'm perfectly all right!

Stasis.

Doris   I think I've had enough for today.

Jackie   Yes, it's getting late, isn't it.

Rosie   It's half past five, you wallies!

Margaret   Rosie, don't shout.

Jackie   Mummy, are you all right?

Doris   I expect she's been overdoing it.

Margaret   Rosie put those baby clothes in the bag for Oxfam.

Rosie   Oh Mum, don't be BORING.

Jackie   Rosie! She's just sitting down.

Rosie   I CAN SEE SHE'S SITTING DOWN!

Doris   You're tired, dear.

Rosie   I'm NOT TIRED!

Jackie   You are!

Rosie   Not you too!

Doris   Margaret, have you seen my piano?

Margaret   It's over there, Mother.

Doris   I KNOW. I'm talking about the polish. You've not even noticed have you?

Margaret   Oh MOTHER! What did you do that for? It'll only need polishing again after the move.

Doris   I'm selling it. At the auction.

Margaret   But it's the only thing Father left for you.

Doris   It was mine anyway. I bought it with my savings from teaching, when I got married. (*Pause.*) You never knew, did you?

Margaret   You can't . . .

Rosie   'Course she can.

Jackie   Food; everyone into the car.

Rosie   I'm not hungry yet.

Margaret   Mother needs to have her tea promptly, don't you dear?

Doris   Oh I'm no trouble. I shall have a boiled egg.

Rosie   Can we go to McDonald's? Yeah!

Jackie   We're all going to my flat.

Margaret   You don't cook, Jackie.

Jackie   We're getting a take-out Indian. There's a good place on the Stockport Road.

Margaret   Mother can't possibly chew spare ribs.

Doris   Chew what?

Rosie   I hate curry. I want a McDonald's. Can I keep these on?

Doris   Yes.

Margaret   No. Have you got your handbag, Mother?

Doris   I don't need helping, thank you. Are you going home in rubber gloves?

Jackie   Mummy, are you OK to drive, if I take the van?

Margaret (*picks up thermos and thermos cup*)   Does anyone want this tea . . . ?

Rosie   Mu-um, it's cold. – Knowing you, you'll probably take it home and save it for tomorrow.

Margaret   Rosie! (*She tips tea into the thermos and screws cup on.*)

Jackie   I'll take these out to the van. (*Goes to the binliners. Sees a dress lying behind them.*) What's this dress? I didn't see it before – it looks like an original 1920s!

Doris   I think there was a tea stain . . . no, it was a grass stain . . . I wore that frock the day that Jack proposed.

Jackie   Do you want to keep it?

Jackie *hesitates, holding up the dress. No response. She puts it in the binliner and ties it shut.*

Margaret   I'm going to check the windows and turn the power off. You two get in the car. (*Exits.*)

Jackie   I'll see you both back at my flat. (*Hesitates.*) Look at you with your hair up like that, Rosie! I wish you were still a baby. You were so sweet . . .

Rosie   Was I?

Doris   There was a time for babies, Jackie, and it's gone.

Rosie   Ow, Jackie you always hug too hard!

Doris   Truth will out, Jackie. Don't say I didn't warn you.

Rosie   C'mon Gran, let's go.

Jackie *looks at* **Doris**, *picks up binliners and goes.*

Doris   Come along Rosie, put your anorak on.

As **Doris** *helps* **Rosie** *into her anorak, the room is suddenly plunged into darkness.*

Doris   Oh!

Rosie   I left the big torch on the landing! – Wait there, Gran. (*Exits.*)

Doris (*goes to French windows. Sound of wind*)   Jack? Ja You should see how the roses have all blown down in garden . . . crushed . . . You rattle like a dry pod, now. Skin on your skull like frayed paper. (*Pause.*) I tried so hard, even in those last few years . . . Something nourishing and not difficult to chew . . . The tray pushed aside on your bed. You did that deliberately, didn't you? (*Pause.*) When you died and the nurses left me alone with you, to pray I suppose, I climbed into bed beside you, yes I did, lay beside you then . . . the sun was shining through the window, hot; only you were cold as ice.

Rosie (*re-enters, carrying a round wooden board; also the flashlight, which she swings around the room until the beam comes to rest on* **Doris**'s *face.* **Doris** *has been crying.*)   − Gran? . . .

Doris   Give me a minute. I'll put my hat and gloves on.

Rosie   Gran? Hurry, what are you doing?

Car horn honks outside.

Doris   Are they waiting for us?

Rosie (*gently*)   You haven't got any gloves . . . oh Gran. (*Goes to* **Doris**. *A split second of hesitation.*)

Doris   Don't kiss −

Rosie   Yes! (**Rosie** *kisses* **Doris**. **Doris** *strokes* **Rosie**'s *hair.*)

Doris   Lovely hair . . . mine are all old grey hairs . . .

Rosie (*holds up a wooden board*)   Look, Gran, look what I found in the spare room. What is it?

Doris   Solitaire. Why, that was my mother's, she gave it me. It's a game. I used to sit and play it in the evenings, while Jack read the papers. You have to get rid of all the marbles from the holes in the board, until there is just one left, in the centre. Solitaire.

Car horn sounds again.

Rosie   Can we take it with us?

Doris   Yes, if you want, Rosie.

Rosie   Will you show me how to do it?

Doris   If you come and visit me. Put your hood up now, it's snowing out.

Rosie *takes the Solitaire board and flashlight. She swings the beam round the room one last time. As they move to go, the sound of wind and snow increases.*

Blackout.

Interval.

Act Three

Scene One

The backyard of **Doris**'s *terrace house in Oldham, early April 1987.* **Doris** *is 87, wears a floral overall;* **Margaret** *is 56, dressed in the sensible suit she wears to work, wearing an apron she has borrowed from* **Doris**. *They are chatting as they come out of the back kitchen door,* **Doris** *guiding* **Margaret**. **Margaret** *is carrying a tray of small geraniums in pots,* **Doris** *carrying a kneeler. They kneel beside a tub and a bag of potting compost.*

Doris   See dear, all those are from the one plant I brought with me from Cheadle Hulme.

Margaret   I've had mine in the kitchen all winter, but they've not done so well.

Doris   Oh you have to cut them right down until they're just dry sticks, then all of a sudden, it seems, they start producing new leaves.

Margaret   They'll look lovely here.

Doris   I've had a postcard from Rosie. She and Jackie seem to be having a lovely time.

Margaret   Yes. It's very quiet at home.

Pause. **Margaret** *continues planting a geranium in the tub.*

Doris   You look thinner. Are you eating properly?

Margaret   What do you mean?

Doris   Don't crowd the roots – Well – you coming all the way from London like this – on a Tuesday!

Margaret   Can't I even come and see you for the day without –

Doris   Usually you're so busy, at that office . . . never have time to come and visit.

Margaret Yes well I took the day off!

Doris No need to snap dear.

Pause. **Margaret** *digs a hole.*

Margaret You've transformed this backyard, I must say. The trellis is nice.

Doris Yes, I'm quite proud, it's only five years since the move. Cheadle Hulme will be a mass of blossom, now, of course. The jasmine hasn't done very well, but then it's been such a spring.

Margaret Good. (*Pause.*) I mean, sorry, yes. – It's been awful, spring, hasn't it.

Doris How are your geranium tubs doing?

Margaret Mmm.

Doris I ate my shoe this afternoon.

Margaret Yes. (*Picks a leaf, stares at it.*)

Doris Margaret, you're not listening to a word I'm saying, are you?

Margaret Of course . . .

Doris What's wrong, Margaret?

Margaret What do you mean, what's wrong?

Doris You're upset.

Margaret I'm probably upset because you're accusing me of being upset.

Doris (*smoothly*) I'm not accusing you. Don't take umbrage.

Margaret Really Mother. I make the effort to come here for a friendly visit and you react as though there's something wrong! Can't I even have a normal conversation with my own Mother?

Doris I don't know, dear.

Margaret   What do you mean, you don't know? (*Pause.*)
And don't call me 'dear'!

Doris   Trains from London are so expensive at this time of
day.

Margaret   There, see? We can't even talk without the
housekeeping coming into it.

Doris (*pause. Gently*)   What is it dear? It's Ken, isn't it
(*Silence.*) . . . He's not been made redundant? (*Silence.*)

Margaret (*pause*)   I don't know.

Doris   What do you mean, you don't know.

Margaret   I haven't seen Ken for a week, Mother. (*Pause.*)
I don't think it's another woman. He's not like that. And
we've always been very happy. I know it happens to one in
three marriages these days, but – you don't think of yourself
as a statistic, do you? (*Pause.*) Mummy, I still want him.

Doris   Your Father . . . stopped 'wanting me', many years
ago. One didn't divorce, then. I thought if I persisted in
loving him . . . I wanted to – to be desired. (*Pause.*) The night
before he died, we embraced. He held my hand; he said that
he loved me most that night. I believed him . . . Was it worth
it, I ask myself? (*Silence.*) You've made more of your life. A
job and that.

Margaret   Exactly. It's all my fault. He loved me, Mother
. . . but he didn't want to share me.

Doris   With who?

Margaret   With the job. Trying to work and look after
Rosie . . . Well I had to work, London's so expensive now.
(*Pause.*) But Ken married a wife, not a working mother.

Doris   You expected too much. So did I. And Jackie
expects even more. (*Pause.*) My father turned up once, after
we'd moved to Jubilee Street. Mother took him back, of
course. I saw the marks, when she was bathing in front of the
fire. She said it was because he loved her so much, he hugged

her too tight. (*Pause*.) When I think about Jack, I think, well, I was lucky really.

Doris *gently lowers the geranium plant into the hole* **Margaret** *has dug.* **Margaret** *pats soil around it.*

Doris   Come in the cottage with me, dear. There's something I want to give you. (*Pause*.) You've never seen a photograph of my Mother, have you?

Margaret (*a white lie*)   No.

Margaret *stands and helps* **Doris** *stand.* **Doris** *takes* **Margaret** *by the arm as they go in.*

Scene Two

Croydon, London, early April 1987, four days later. A bright sunny morning in **Margaret**'s *office, but traffic noise outside. A desk, a telephone, a typewriter, a pot of geraniums and a photo frame.* **Margaret** *is 56,* **Jackie** *is 34,* **Rosie** *is 15½.*

Margaret   *is seated, uncovering the typewriter. She wears a sensible suit as in the previous scene.*

Rosie (*enters with an orange kite and a bundle of letters, which she puts on* **Margaret**'s *desk. She wears colourful and sophisticated holiday clothes*)   Morning post, Mrs Metcalfe.

Margaret   Rosie! What on earth are you doing here?

Rosie (*kisses* **Margaret**. *Makes the kite swoop round the office space*   Look! Isn't it beautiful!

Margaret   Have you been home yet?

Rosie   No. We came straight from Gatwick, all the way in a taxi, can you imagine! But Jackie says when it's important you have to do these things.

Margaret (*touching her hair*)   Is she here too?

Rosie   Yes. Only she's gone in the third floor Ladies to change into her Art Dealer dress. She doesn't want you to see her looking a mess.

Margaret   Is she going straight back to work?

Rosie   There's some meeting about the future of her gallery, with the Manchester City Council. (*She swoops the kite.*)

Margaret   But you've both been travelling all night!

Rosie   So?

Margaret   You'd better get that out of sight before Mr Reece arrives at nine.

Rosie   Don't you like it? Such style, the Italians.

Margaret   How was Venice?

Rosie   Brilliant! 'Fettucine alla casa, va bene?'! The food was marvellous. Dad would have hated it!

Margaret   I'm sure.

Rosie   I can't believe it's only two weeks! What have you been up to? You didn't clean my room?

Margaret   I went to visit Granny.

Rosie   I sent her a postcard of the beach where we flew this kite. Also we brought some Chianti back for Dad, and you'll never guess what we've brought you! Did Dad water my tomatoes?

Margaret (*pause*)   Dad's gone away for the week. What did you like best in Venice?

Rosie   Oh, definitely the carnival. We stayed up all night, everyone wore masks like birds, that's when I saw the kites. We had breakfast at San Marco's, and this man fell in love with Jackie, so I just stared into the canal and ordered another cappucino, and pretended I was waiting for a gondola. And then it turned out it was me he fancied, and Jackie got very cross with him in Italian, and we had to leave.

Margaret   I hope you didn't stay up every night?

Rosie   Oh yes – Mum, of course not. I mean – Jackie's so sweet, she was trying so hard to be like you.

Margaret   Like me?

Rosie   Yes. I can't think of anyone less like a mother!
(*Pause.*) You know Mum, sometimes you have to be a bit silly
with Jackie just to get her to relax. She needs . . .

Margaret   What does she need?

Rosie   . . . I don't know . . . it's hard to explain. (*Thinks.*)
She's so restless: she's always looking for something to do. We
spent a whole day trekking round museums but she could
never find the picture she wanted. After I'd got this kite, we
went to this incredible long beach, ran for miles. (*Swoops
kite.*) We were shouting because of the wind, and Jackie got
the kite to do a perfect circle in the sky . . . Oh Mum, it was
such a brilliant day . . . Will you stop opening letters for a
minute –

Margaret   I'm at work.

Rosie   Yes, but I have to tell you something! Oh Mum, it's
incredible!

Margaret   What dear?

Rosie   Well, I asked Jackie – I could't believe she'd agree –
I want to go and live with her in Manchester!

Margaret (*long pause*)   What about your exams?

Rosie   Oh, I won't go till the summer, of course. Anyway,
Jackie says we have to discuss it with you and Dad first.
(*Pause.*) Mum . . . ?

Margaret   You've no idea. Jackie can't cook, she'll forget
to wash your clothes . . .

Rosie   I know! She's so useless at most things. Not like you.
(*Pause.*) She needs me. (*Pause.*) I'll come back and visit, lots.

Margaret   Whenever you can afford the fare.

Rosie   Oh Jackie will pay. She says we'll both visit. She
comes to London all the time, anyway.

Margaret   Does she?

Rosie (*cuts in*)   You said! Don't you remember? You promised, after my exams I could do whatever I wanted.

Margaret (*long pause*)   Yes, I did. (*Turns away, afraid she's going to cry.*) I've got to . . . write a letter, Rosie, can you wait outside a minute . . .

Rosie exits, swooping the kite as she goes. **Jackie** *and* **Rosie** *meet in the corridor.* **Jackie** *is wearing a print dress, carrying a Chinese lacquered briefcase and a blue kite.*

Rosie   Don't go in. (*Surveys* **Jackie**.) You've spoiled it now, Miss Executive. You should go to work wearing that turquoise thing.

Jackie   That was a beach dress.

Rosie   Suited you much better.

Jackie   It's an incredibly important meeting.

Rosie   All the more reason to let them see what you're really like.

Jackie   I can't start now.

Rosie   You could. If you really wanted. Come outside and fly this kite with me.

Jackie   I want to see Mummy.

Rosie   She's busy.

Jackie   I'll sit in her office and prepare for my meeting.

Rosie   See – now you're being all business woman again!

Jackie   Calm down. You're not at home now.

Rosie   Mum isn't like you when she's at work. (*Goes, swooping the kite.*)

Jackie (*enters the office*)   Mummy! I'm sorry. Didn't you get the message? The delay was twelve hours in the end, airport like an oven.

Margaret   Rosie's hopelessly over-excited.

Jackie   I know Mummy, I couldn't get her to sleep. But she's been so good all holiday, you don't need to worry. She's very sensible for fifteen. Wouldn't let me swim too far out.

Margaret   She'll be tired for the first day of term now.

Jackie   That's three days away!

Margaret   There's all her clothes to wash.

Jackie   I'd do it, but I've . . .

Margaret   Got to go back to Manchester for a meeting.

Jackie (*pause*)   Rosie can wash her own things. She did all our clothes one evening, fixed up a line on the balcony.

Margaret   It's an adventure with you. (*Pause.*) You should see her bedroom, it's like a junkyard – clothes, glue, paint.

Jackie   She's very creative. Kept writing poetry in the restaurant.

Margaret   She's full of crazy ideas. (*Testing* **Jackie**.)

Jackie (*pause. Cautious*)   Is she? (*No reply from* **Margaret**.) It's just her energy, isn't it . . . ?

Margaret (*pause*)   Well of course with you – (*Stops.*)

Jackie   She talks about you a lot.

Margaret   What about?

Jackie   Oh, I only mean your job. She wanted to show me all round where you work.

Margaret   Did she?

Jackie   You didn't tell me you were promoted last year. (*Looks over* **Margaret**'s *shoulder at the letters she is opening.*)

Margaret   It's nothing glamorous.

Jackie   You know I'd be useless at this. My typing's awful . . . Do you have to reply to all these?

Margaret   Mr Reece dictates, I spend the rest of the morning unravelling his grammar, otherwise British

Microwaves would never have any export trade. These young graduates.

Jackie   I hope they pay you the right scale. You're the one who does all the work.

Margaret   I'm only his personal assistant.

Jackie   Don't say 'only'.

Margaret   Oh I was lucky. My typing speeds are very ordinary. It's only that I've got Pitman's Classic and most of the girls don't learn shorthand these days.

Jackie   I'm sure it's other qualities got you this job, Mummy.

Margaret (*pause. Pleased*)   It's funny, hearing 'Mummy' in this place. You do a job, people treat you differently.

Jackie   It's only how you treat yourself.

Margaret (*pause*)   You look radiant dear.

Jackie   Swimming and sea air. (*Quiet.*) Bit of sun, Mummy. Do you good, too.

Margaret (*quiet*)   Sat in the garden this weekend. Been very . . . Been a relief, you having Rosie for these two weeks.

Jackie (*pause*)   I hope you kept the appointment? She's a nice woman, isn't she?

Margaret   It was a very expensive looking waiting room.

Jackie   Mummy, I asked you to see the specialist, not the wallpaper. What did she say?

Margaret   Oh – Nothing much.

Jackie   Did she do some tests?

Margaret   No.

Jackie   No?

Margaret   Says I'm fine. Just menopause, probably.

Jackie (*pause*)   Honestly?

Margaret (*pause*)   What do you mean?

Jackie Well – (*Pause.*) – That's such a relief! (*Laughs.*) Oh Mummy. We even got a taxi all the way here!

Margaret (*pause*) Now you can go and catch your train to Manchester, can't you.

Jackie Mum . . . May bank holiday, come and stay with me. Just you, and we'll . . .

Margaret Fly kites.

Jackie (*gives her the blue kite*) Oh yes, Rosie and I bought you a kite. She says Daddy will show you how to fly it, but I said you're an expert. Do you remember, how you took me flying kites in Richmond Park, and once it got stuck in a chestnut tree, and all the conkers came down?

Margaret I thought you'd wiped out that little girl.

Jackie So did I. Rosie won't. She'll have kites in her office, or whatever. (*Pause.*) I used to wear suits, when I first started my job. (*Bends and picks up a photo frame*) Is this Cornwall? . . . Oh can I have a copy? Doesn't Rosie look sweet!

Margaret (*pause*) Rosie's told me, Jackie.

Jackie (*terrified*) I wasn't going to –

Margaret No, I expect you had another date planned when you were going to tell me that you'd like Rosie back. Or perhaps you were just going to tell me over the phone.

Jackie . . . You need time, to decide . . . in the summer –

Margaret It's not my decision. It's Rosie's. And she's made her mind up. (*Pause.*) I knew she'd say it one day. Like one of those fairy tales.

Jackie You haven't told her!

Margaret Of course not. She still thinks you're big sister, that's why it's so magical to her.

Jackie We were running along this dazzling beach. I thought, is that what I've missed?

Margaret   Years and years and years you've lost, Jackie. Birthdays and first snowman and learning to ride a bicycle and new front teeth. You can't pull them back.

Jackie   I can make up for it – somehow –

Margaret   You can't. Those are my years.

Jackie   She must remember – I visited!

Margaret   Treats, she's had with you. A day here and there. That never fooled her. But I let it fool you. I'm the woman who sat up all night with the sick child, who didn't mind all her best crockery getting broken over the years.

Jackie   Mummy . . .

Margaret (*long pause. Cool*)   What time's your train?

Jackie   9.45 – no – I could get the 10.45.

Margaret   You mustn't miss your meeting.

Jackie   It would give us another hour. I wish we weren't in your office! (*Panics.*) Where's Rosie gone?

Margaret   Are you going to catch that train, or stay here? You can't do both.

Pause. **Jackie** *agonises.*

Margaret   I'll phone you a taxi. (**Margaret** *dials, waits, the line is engaged.*)

Jackie (*quietly*)   You know Mummy, the Gallery and everything, I couldn't have done it without you. You can't be a mother and then cancel Christmas to be in New York.

Margaret (*telephone connects*)   Taxi to East Croydon station please, immediately. British Microwaves, front entrance. (*Puts receiver down.*)

Jackie   Come and stay, show me how you do things, how Rosie would like her room decorated.

Margaret   No Jackie, I shall just put a label around Rosie's neck, and send her Red Star. (*Doesn't look at* **Jackie**

any more, busies herself with papers.) It's gone nine. I wonder where Mr Reece is?

Jackie *runs out of the room.*

Margaret (*bursts into tears. Telephone rings*)   Hello? Hello. Yes, I'll be with you directly. (*Puts down the receiver.*) Oh God, my mascara – all over the letters. (*Picks up notebook to go.*) It will be strange. I'm a single woman again. (*Calms herself.*) I'll oversleep. (*Hesitates then dials telephone.*) Hello? Manchester City Art Gallery? Yes, I'd like to leave a message for Jackie Metcalfe. Just say – (*Pause.*) – May bank holiday will be fine. (*Puts phone down and walks out of the office. Blackout.*)

Scene Three

The Wasteland. Cats wail. Almost dark. We see the glint of faces and hands.

Jackie   Harelip and eye of bat.

Rosie   Poisoned dewdrop and tail of cat.

Jackie   Put it in a monkey's hat.

Doris   What's a monkey's hat?

Jackie   Sssh!

Rosie   You can't have harelip.

Jackie   Sssh!

Doris   Why?

Rosie   It's something real. You get it. I've seen a lady with it in the opticians.

Doris   What's it like?

Jackie   Sssh! I can't con-centrate. This is a laboratory. (*Stirring twig potage.*)

Rosie   It's a sort of slit in your mouth, goes up your nose.

Doris   Eugh.

Rosie   You're born with it. It means you're missing a bit in the head, too.

Jackie   Shut up!

Doris   Let's go and have a look!

Rosie   Optician's closed.

Jackie   (*mysteriously*)   She didn't used to have it. It grew.

Rosie   Honest?

Jackie   Maybe *we* did it. (*Pause.*)

Rosie   How could we . . .

Doris   Could we?

Jackie   (*grand*)   I can tell you what her name is.

Rosie   Go on.

Jackie   Mrs Worsley.

Doris   That's right!

Jackie   See? Proves it. Our powers.

Doris   What powers?

Jackie   In the earth.

Rosie   What happens to people when they die, then?

Jackie   They rot. Worms go in their nose and out their eyeballs.

Doris   No! (*Starts to cry.*) I don't want to do that—

Jackie   It's too late.

Rosie   I don't want to do that to Mum!

Jackie   'S too late. Was her idea.

Doris   No!

Rosie   No it wasn't, it was yours.

Doris   Stop it!

Rosie   Stop the spell.

Doris Make it go backwards!

Jackie You can't make someone's life go backwards.

Rosie I'm going to tell her – c'mon! (*Grabs* **Doris** *and they run off.*)

Doris Wasn't me!

Jackie She'll be dead when you get there.

Cats wail. The shadowy figure of **Margaret** *appears upstage.*

Jackie I didn't mean to do it! Don't leave me all alone!

She runs off.

Scene Four

Hospital, Twickenham, late May 1987. **Margaret** *in a hospital gown, with her hair scraped back. Her face is drawn, and very white. Under anaesthetic. She has become only a voice.*

Margaret I know the door is here somewhere, if only I could find it, the door to the garden . . . Here's a door . . . the bathroom! . . . What a cold wind blowing through here . . . Why, here we are, on its iron legs, the white enamel bath . . . cold on your bare flesh, even in summer . . . goosepimples . . . Father's made his fortune! But we still have to save hot water . . . Everything is a sacrifice in this house. Everything – is – sacrified for . . . Piano Tuition.
Tu-ition . . . BUT! (*Whispers, conspiratorial.*) One must go to the bathroom and lock the door if one wants – needs – to CRY! . . . When you pull the plug out, the water gets sucked down with a roar . . . So they know I'm here . . . no privacy in this huge house . . . My parents are called, My parents are called . . . Guilt and Duty . . . When *I* have babies, they will be called Sugar and Spice and all things nice . . . I will give them everything they want, and they will love me (*Pause.*) . . . Mother? . . . Mummy . . . What happens when you die? . . . I wish they wouldn't keep opening the door, it's so cold . . . I'm sure I can find the garden, if I just keep going.

Lights fade on her. We hear a child crying, then a baby crying. Fade out.

Scene Five

*The garden of **Ken** and **Margaret**'s suburban semi in Raynes Park, London, late May 1987, early morning, two hours after Scene Four. **Rosie** sits on the swing beneath the cherry tree with the old red tranny wearing one of **Ken**'s jumpers, which is much too big, and jeans. **Jackie** runs across the garden, hot and grubby, carrying her lacquered briefcase, dressed for work. Both have been up all night.*

LBC Radio   More congestion on the North Circular, meanwhile the overturned tanker is still blocking the Blackwall Tunnel. And it's coming up to eight o'clock, a lovely May morning . . . Looking down the Euston Road, here's to the girl in that blue Mini, a thought from the Beatles . . . (*Plays 'All You Need Is Love'.*)

Jackie   Rosie? . . .

*Silence. Hold this for as long as possible while **Jackie** has to cope with it.*

Rosie   I hope you're a success, Jackie. A big, big success.

Jackie   Rosie are you all right? Where's Daddy?

Rosie   I hope lots of people came to your opening and thought your gallery was brill.

Jackie   It was only twelve hours – I'd never have gone back to Manchester if I'd thought – after Daddy phoned last night, there were no more planes. I got the first plane I could this morning. If only . . .

Rosie   In case you want to know, she died at 6.20 last night. Dad was with her. They said it was quicker at the end. It wasn't just stomach cancer, there were secondaries.

Jackie (*goes to hug **Rosie** who won't let her*)   If only I'd been here with you . . .

Rosie (*turns away*)   Did you sell lots of your paintings?

Jackie Rosie –

Rosie Did you?

Jackie I didn't sell any. I cancelled the opening.

Rosie I don't believe you. You'd never do that.

Silence.

Jackie What do we do . . . now? . . . I'll call a taxi to the hospital – do we have to take things – her birth certificate? . . . I don't know . . .

Rosie Dad's done all that. He's been brilliant, like it was before they split up. He knew where Mum kept the box that's got all the family stuff in it. Look – he said I could have this one – (*Holds out a photo.*) That's Mum holding me by the front door when I'd just arrived . . . And . . . (*Lays them on grass.*) – Here's Mum's birth certificate, . . . and here's mine.

Silence.

Jackie No.

Rosie So now I know.

Jackie (*desperate*) I was going to tell you – in five months – when you were sixteen . . . Mummy said to wait till after your exams, so as not to upset you . . .

Rosie (*has a handful of photos, throws them down one by one, except for one which she slips in her pocket*) 1972, my first birthday, 1973, my second birthday, Christmas 1975, 1976; then you were in South America, 1979 with the birthday cake, 1982 when we cleared Gran and Grandad's house, – and our holiday in Venice. (*Pause.*) Have them. Have them all.

Jackie Rosie – we've got to help each other now.

Rosie Why don't you go and get drunk, or whatever it is you lot do to show you're feeling something.

Jackie I wanted you to have opportunities I couldn't ever have given you.

Rosie No you didn't. You wanted your own life more than you wanted mine!

e Don't!

ie If you were really my Mum you wouldn't have been able to give me away!

Jackie How dare you! (*Goes to hit* **Rosie** *but cannot.*) You're at the centre of everything I do! (*Slight pause.*) Mummy treated me as though I'd simply fallen over and cut my knee, – picked me up and said you'll be all right now, it won't show much. She wanted to make it all better. (*Quiet.*) . . . She was the one who wanted it kept secret . . . I WANTED you, Rosie. (*Angry.*) For the first time in my life I took care of myself – refused joints, did exercises, went to the clinic. (*Pause.*) 'It's a girl'. (*Smiles irresistibly.*) – After you'd gone I tried to lose that memory. (*Pause. Effort.*) Graham . . . your Father. (*Silence.*) He couldn't be there the day you were born, he had to be in Liverpool. He was married. (*Emphatic.*) He loved me, he loved you, you must believe that! (*Pause.*) He said he'd leave his wife, but I knew he wouldn't; there were two children, the youngest was only four . . . we'd agreed, separate lives, I wanted to bring you up. He sent money. (*Pause.*) I took you to Lyme Park one day, I saw them together, across the lake, he was buying them ice creams, his wife was taking a photo. I think they live in Leeds now, I saw his name in the Guardian last year, an article about his photographs . . . (*Pause.*) It was a very cold winter after you were born. There were power cuts. I couldn't keep the room warm; there were no lights in the tower blocks; I knew he had an open fire, it was trendy; so we took a bus to Didsbury, big gardens, pine kitchens, made a change from concrete. I rang the bell. (*Stops.*) A Punjabi man answered, said he was sorry . . . they'd moved. By the time we got back to Mosside it was dark, the lift wasn't working – (*Stops.*) That was the night I phoned Mummy. (*Difficult.*) Asked her. (*Pause.*) I tried! I couldn't do it, Rosie. (*Pause.*) It doesn't matter how much you succeed afterwards, if you've failed once. (*Pause.*) After you'd gone . . . I kept waking in the night to feed you . . . A week . . . in the flat . . . Then I went back to art school. Sandra and Hugh thought I was inhuman. I remember the books that came out that winter – how to succeed as a single working mother – fairy tales! (*Pause.*) Sandra and Hugh have a family now. Quite a few of my friends do. (*Pause.*) I could give you everything now. Rosie? . . .

Rosie (*pause*)   I used to hate you, only I never knew why. (*Gestures.*) Sit down on the swing. I'm going to Oldham, to live with Gran – Great-Gran. Dad says I can.

Jackie (*hesitates*)   I'm frightened.

Rosie   Sit down on the swing (*She holds the ropes.*) Put your head back and look up through the cherry tree. The sky is falling. Mum used to sit here with me in her arms, and I'd pretend I was asleep. I'm never having any children. (*Starts towards the house.*)

Jackie   You might.

Rosie *hears, but keeps walking away.*

Lights fade to blackout.

Scene Six

The Wasteground.

Margaret *walks in, balancing on cracks of paving.*

Margaret   King of the Golden River! (*Demonstrates invisible line.*) I'm the King.

Jackie (*runs in*)   Farmer Farmer, may I cross your golden river, just to take our Daddy's dinner.

Jackie *runs to cross the line,* **Margaret** *chases and catches her.*

Margaret   You've got to do a dare . . . !

Jackie   I've been in the boys' den . . .

Margaret   And?

Jackie   They wanted me to kill you.

Margaret   It didn't work.

Jackie   Sure?

Margaret   Yes.

Slight pause.

Jackie   The others won't play with me any more.

Margaret   Tell you what.

Jackie   What?

Margaret   You can come with me. To my secret, secret hide.

Margaret *holds out her hand.* **Jackie** *takes it.*

Jackie   No. Not yet. Do you mind?

Margaret *shakes her head.* **Jackie** *lets go of her hand and walks away. The lights start to fade on* **Margaret***, who stands watching until* **Jackie** *is out of sight.* **Margaret** *resumes balancing along the cracks in the paving. The lights fade to blackout during:*

Margaret   King of the Golden River . . . I'm the King.

Scene Seven

Oldham, September 1987. The backyard of **Doris***'s end terrace cottage. Distant sound of children. Two deck chairs. Piano stool from Act One, on it the Solitaire board from Act Two. A tub of geraniums. A green kite.* **Rosie** *is sunbathing in shorts and painted T-shirt, both of which she has tie-dyed herself, and she is wearing Walkman headphones, oblivious of all other noise. She hums Simply Red's 'Holding Back The Years', as she concentrates on the Solitaire game.*

Doris   (*appears upstage, holding up kite tail. Calls*)   Is this right?

Rosie   (*hums*)   . . . Holding back the years . . .

Doris   (*comes nearer*)   Rosie? CAN YOU HEAR ME DEAR? (*Taps* **Rosie** *on the shoulder.*)

Rosie   SORRY! (*Removes headphones.*)

Doris   You're shouting again, dear. Neighbours will think I'm deaf. (*Holds up kite tail.*) Is this right?

Rosie   Looks great! Thanks. (*Picks up the kite.*) Here, just tie it on the bottom.

Doris (*ties the kite tail to the kite*)   Needs a stitch in it . . .

Rosie (*holds the kite aloft*)   What d'you think?

Doris (*pause*)   I preferred the blue ones.

Rosie   Well they've ordered fifty, so I'm not complaining. (*Puts the kite down.*) Did ten this morning.

Doris   I gathered that, from the state of the box room. Bits of string . . .

Rosie   It's not for you to clear up. Sit down Doris, enjoy the sun.

Doris (*sits*)   I fancy one of those garden tables . . . white ones, with an umbrella. But they do cost, don't they?

Rosie (*firmly*)   When I've sold the next batch, maybe. We mustn't spend before we've paid off the overheads.

Doris   You shouldn't be bothering your head with work on your birthday. (*Pause.*) Just like your mother.

Rosie   Did you see her present!

Doris   Mrs W saw me take it in. Postman couldn't get it through the letterbox.

Rosie   It's one of her paintings.

Doris   I propped it on the mantelpiece.

Rosie   What d'you think?

Doris (*pause*)   I liked the gold frame. Looks expensive.

Rosie   Gran! She did it specially for me.

Rosie *returns to Solitaire.*

Doris   Is Jackie still seeing that man with the hairdo?

Rosie   Dreadlocks. You mean Andy, yeah. Think he's OK.

Doris   D'you think she'll marry?

Rosie   Last time I was with them they bought a duvet.
They go shopping together.

Doris   Like us.

Rosie   You promised you'd show me how to do the
Solitaire, today.

Doris   You work it out. (*She watches* **Rosie** *for a moment.*) No
cheating, mind. Took my Mother years to work it out. She
showed me, but she made me vow never to tell anyone. I
didn't even tell Jack, and husbands and wives aren't
supposed to have any secrets, are they?

Rosie   Listen, I've been trying all week, and I can't do it.

Doris   One week is nothing.

Rosie *studies the board.*

Doris   Isn't this sunshine cheering? (*She puts on a pair of
mirrored sunglasses.*)

Rosie   What do you think my next move should be?

Doris   What do you think, Rosie?

Rosie (*laughs*)   Oh Doris, take my shades off!

Doris   They're mine. Bought them at the checkout when I
went for the ice cream.

Rosie   There's a new Pakistani shop opened. Even cheaper
than Kwiksave.

Doris   Jack came home one night and I was sat in the dark.
I told him, I'm economising. He said, that's just as well, you
left the hall light on. (*Pause.*) You can't win.

Rosie   You can. Look, double jump! Is that allowed?

Doris   Yes. Do you know, I think I'll even take my
stockings off, and then my legs can brown. (*Modestly reaches
under her skirt and unhooks her stockings.*) Well, I may be as old as
the Queen Mother, but *I* buy all my smalls in Top Shop.

Rosie   Hmmm . . . (*Removes another marble.*)

Doris Do you know Rosie, there's no such snob as the snob who rises from the gutter . . .

Rosie Are you 'casting aspersions' again? Grubbing at the Royal Family this time, are you?

Doris No. As a matter of fact I was making an inference to my late husband. Jack would never have tolerated this lack of modesty in a woman. (*Pause.*) Although while we're on the subject, it is true that the Queen Mother was a Commoner before she married up.

Rosie AH! Triple jump! Fucking brill!

Doris Does one have to lower the tone of the afternoon quite so crudely?

Rosie Stop attempting posh, Doris. Your slip is showing.

Doris Is it? . . . Still, I don't suppose the Queen Mother does all her own washing . . . (*Leans back and closes her eyes.*)

Rosie *puts headphones back on. Hums.*

A lull.

Doris I suppose now you've got hold of that game, I won't be hearing from you till the Christmas after next.

Rosie (*singing softly. Moves a marble*) Ah!

Doris (*opens her eyes*) What with that electronic earmuff you wear, night and day.

Rosie (*studying the board*) Hmm . . .

Doris In my day, families practised the art of conversation.

Rosie Aah! (*Removes another marble.*)

Doris (*watches* **Rosie** *fondly*) Your mother couldn't solve that. Though she tried.

Rosie (*removes headphones*) Are you talking to me? (*Stretches.*) Mmm! It's hot, like being inside a blue balloon. (*Gazes out.*) The moors are clear today. We should've walked up to the Waterloo Memorial.

Doris (*gazes out*)   Wicked, sticking these tower blocks in the view.

Rosie   It's so lovely here, Doris. (*Pause.*) Ken phoned to say happy birthday. I asked him to put some flowers on Margaret's grave today.

Doris (*pause*)   To think, Jack and I in this same street, sixty years ago – scrimping and saving so that our child would have a better start in life . . . You do what you believe is best for your daughter, you know Rosie, and then you find it wasn't what she wanted. Or needed.

Rosie   Remember what Jackie said afterwards. We mustn't live in the past.

Doris   Well I don't see that I've much of a future. Stuck here with my great-granddaughter in a two-up, two-down.

Rosie   Gran!

Doris (*winding her up*)   Forced to do piecework, tying scraps of coloured paper to lengths of string all day long . . .

Rosie   How much do you want that garden table . . . ?

Doris   You fancy you can bribe your great-grandmother?

Rosie   Yes.

Doris (*pause*)   How many did you say you wanted?

Rosie   Fifty. By the end of the week. We can do them sitting out here.

Doris   'Campaign Kites' . . . Who'd have thought you'd earn a living off them. (**Rosie** *moves another marble.*) Who are they for this time?

Rosie   Greenpeace.

Doris   Had another phone call from that Animal Liberation man.

Rosie   I won't do business with organisations that use violence. (*Pause.*) What did you tell him?

Doris   That he was politically unsound.

Rosie   That's a good phrase.

Doris   Heard a girl say it at the evening class.

Rosie   Let me guess . . . Tricia?

Doris   No – a new girl in Women's Literature – She's from the tower block over there. I've met her in the Welfare with her two babbies, and do you know, she doesn't look the sort to even open a book. But she's quite the best, the comments she comes out with in class. She can't spell, of course. (*Pause.*) But it just goes to show: you can't judge by appearances. Jack was wrong. (*Pause.*) Even so, I do wish you wouldn't wear those dirty rags. You look . . . like a victim.

Rosie   I made this T-shirt. It got ripped at the last march. Perhaps someone will find it in our cellar one day, and remember. (*Pause.*) And remember me.

Doris   At least you're not wounded inside.

Pause.

Rosie (*removes another marble*)   . . . Look, this is a magic marble: when you hold it up to the sun there's a frozen fountain inside.

Doris   It seems no time since you were trying to push that up your nose. (*Pause.*) I'm going to put our tea on. Can you pass my shoes?

Rosie   I'll do it.

Doris   No, it really is my turn.

Rosie   – Have you got me a birthday cake!

Doris   Yes.

Rosie   I love you, Doris.

Doris   A long time since anyone's said that to me. (*Pause.*) Sixty-one years, Jack and I were married. I don't think we liked each other very much. (*Pause.*) There's a letter here for you.

Rosie   There's no address on it.

Doris   It's from your mother. I've kept it safe in my
scrapbox, with Jack's letters, and Margaret's exercise book,
and the drawings Jackie did when she was a little girl.
(*Pause.*) After Margaret took you to London, Jackie came to
see me. Left some baby clothes, and asked me to give you this
letter when you reached sixteen. Happy Birthday. (*Kisses*
Rosie. *Goes in to the cottage.*)

Rosie *picks up the letter, opens it and reads.*

Rosie   '. . . I don't know if you'll ever love me as much as I
love you. But one day you'll understand why I've done this to
you, probably not until you are on your own yourself . . .'
(**Rosie** *throws the letter down. After a moment she retrieves it. She
concentrates on the Solitaire board and completes the game with a few
last moves, so that one marble is left in the centre hole.*) Solitaire!
(*Calls.*) Gran! Gran, guess what, I've discovered the secret,
all by myself! Gran? I'll prove it to you, come and watch, I'm
going to do it all over again now, so that I remember it
always. You there Gran? (*Silence.*) Oh never mind.

Rosie *puts the headphones back on and hums quietly. As she replaces
all the marbles on the board,* **Jackie** *appears upstage, dressed as in Act
Three, Scene Five.* **Margaret** *appears also, dressed as in Act Three,
Scene Two. The blue kite flies up high over* **Margaret**.

Scene Eight

Enter **Doris** *in the 1920s print dress which* **Jackie** *pulled from the
box in Act Two and a straw hat trimmed with flowers. She is breathless
and her hair is awry. Oldham, May 1923.*

Doris   Mother! Mother? Oh, what do you think! It's
happened, happened to me! All the way back on the train I
could hardly keep still; I don't know what the other
passengers must've thought, but I wouldn't be ladylike.
Mother! Come and look. Do I look different? I must look
different, I feel as though I've swallowed a firework. Oh it
was a lovely, lovely day. We took a picnic, climbed up to the
Waterloo Memorial, sat in the sunshine and it was after we'd

finished the egg and cress; he couldn't wait till after the fruit cake! I felt so – shy, suddenly – I had to just stare and stare at the tablecloth while he was asking, blue and yellow squares, there was an ant struggling to carry a piece of cress across the corner . . . These are things you remember all your life, I suppose. I didn't think it would be like this. (*Pause.*) And then we just ran and ran! Talked, made plans, I felt somehow – weedy! (*Laughs.*) – Sort of silly, for having given in . . . to – love! – Do you know what I mean? (*Silence.*) Mother? We ate your fruit cake on the train. Jack put a paper down so as not to drop crumbs on the velvet upholstery, but then he sat on a strawberry – and oh, I got a grass stain on my frock, but Jack says he'll buy me a new one. *And*, Mother, *and* I got promoted to Head of Infants this morning! Miss Butterworth called me into her office, my heart was in my mouth, I thought she was going to tick me off for this dress being too short! . . . Jack was very proud when I told him, but of course he says I shan't need to work when we're – when we're – oh, of course he's going to ask you first, he's waiting in the front room, I opened the curtains so the neighbours can see – Oh and – (*Lights begin to fade.*) I've seen just the posy, tiny white flowers, in the window of Ambleton's . . . Oh Mother, I'm so happy, SO HAPPY! I suppose, really and truly, this is the beginning of my life! (*Lights fade to a single spot on* **Doris**, *then snap out.*)

Solution to the Solitaire Game

For Rosie in Act Three, Scene Seven.

A Solitaire board (see diagram on p. 95) looks much like a round wooden bread board, with a groove running round just inside the rim where discarded marbles are put. There are thirty-three holes on the board. Initially these are all filled with marbles except for the centre hole which is empty. The game is to clear the board leaving one marble in the centre hole. The rule is that a marble can only be moved by hopping it over another marble, up or down or across but not diagonally. The static marble which has been hopped over, is then removed from its hole and discarded.

For the scene, Rosie only needs the last eleven marbles on the board. She can then pace the final moves through the scene with Doris. There are no numbers on a Solitare board, but the diagram has been numbered for clarity. As can be seen, the following holes have marbles in them: five, nine, eleven, fifteen, seventeen, nineteen, twenty-one, twenty-two, twenty-four, twenty-six, twenty-seven.

The ten moves are as follows and each marble that is hopped over is removed from the board, while the hopping marble lands in a new hole.

   1. Marble from *twenty-one* jumps over marble in *twenty-two* and into hole *twenty-three*

   2. Marble from *twenty-seven* jumps over marble in *twenty-six* and into hole *twenty-five*

   3. Marble from *twenty-four* jumps over marble in *twenty-three* and into hole *twenty-two*

   4. Marble from *twenty-two* jumps over marble in *fifteen* and into hole *eight*

   5. Marble from *eight* jumps over marble in *nine* and into hole *ten*

   6. Marble from *ten* jumps over marble in *eleven* and into hole *twelve*

   7. Marble from *twelve* jumps over marble in *nineteen* and into hole *twenty-six*

8. Marble from *twenty-six* jumps over marble in *twenty-five* and into hole *twenty-four*

9. Marble from *twenty-four* jumps over marble in *seventeen* and into hole *ten*

10. Marble from *five* jumps over marble in *ten* and into hole *seventeen*

The marble for the third move (from hole twenty-four) continues hopping through the next six moves. Therefore, when Rosie says 'double jump' or 'triple jump', what she is doing is playing the third to seventh moves as a sequence. The actress can delay picking up the hopped over marbles each time so as to prolong these moves. The stage directions indicate (*She removes a marble.*) every so often, as a rough guide. The actress can pace it as she wants, and add extra marbles if she wants more moves. At the point Doris leaves Rosie with the letter, Rosie should have four marbles left on the board, ready for the eighth, ninth and tenth moves. These are the moves with which Rosie completes the game alone and ends with one marble in the centre hole – seventeen. Solitaire!

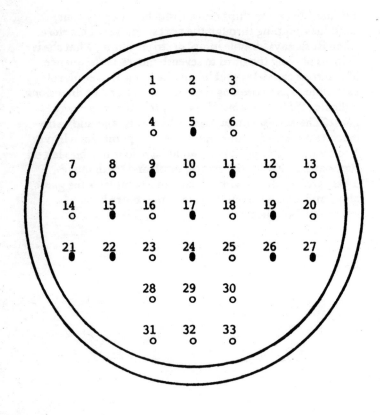